THE
BACKWATERS
PRESS

GRACE BAUER

UNHOLY HEART

New and Selected Poems

The Backwaters Press
An imprint of the University of Nebraska Press

Library of Congress Control Number: 2020035406

Set in Adobe Caslon Pro by Mikala R. Kolander.
Designed by L. Auten.

This book is dedicated to my family and to the friends who have helped make life both holier and unholier—and a helluva lot more fun

And to the memory of my father—Frank "Fats" Bauer

CONTENTS

ACKNOWLEDGMENTS

Previously published books:

The Women at the Well (Portals Press, 1996; Stephen F. Austin
State University Press, 2016)

Retreats & Recognitions (Lost Horse Press, 2007)

Beholding Eye (CustomWords, 2006)

Nowhere All At Once (Stephen F. Austin State University Press, 2014)

MEAN/TIME (University of New Mexico Press, 2017)

Some of these poems also previously appeared in these chapbooks:

Where You've Seen Her

The House Where I've Never Lived

Field Guide to the Ineffable: Poems on Marcel Duchamp

Café Culture

My gratitude to the editors of the journals and anthologies where
many of these poems—sometimes in different form—originally
appeared.

Journals

*American Literary Review, Apalachee Quarterly, Artemis, Arts & Letters,
Bat City Review, Berkeley Poets' Cooperative, Bosque (the magazine),
Comstock Review, Connotations Press: An Online Artifact, Cricket, Dou-
bletake, Four Corners, Frontiers: A Journal of Women's Studies, Gargoyle,
Georgetown Review, Grist, Iowa Woman, Iris, The Journal, Lake Effect,
The MacGuffin, Margie, Measure, Nebraska Life, New Madrid, North
American Review, North Carolina Humanities, Outerbridge, Paterson*

Poetry Review, Permafrost, Pinyon, Poetry, Puerto del Sol, Rattle, Route Nine, Route 7 Review, Shenandoah, Slant, South Dakota Review, Southern Poetry Review, Terrain, Xavier Review

Anthologies

"Nowhere All At Once," "Geography Lessons," "Latter Day Saints," *Times of Sorrow, Times of Grace*

"Note from the Imaginary Daughter," *The Muse Strikes Back*

"Eve Recollecting the Garden," *Other Testaments: A Poetry Anthology*

"Eve Recollecting the Garden," *Literature: An Introduction to Critical Reading*

"Her Great Escape," *Sampler*

Poems from this manuscript were also featured in *American Life in Poetry, Poetry Daily, This American Life, Verse Daily, and Women's Voices for Change*.

Thanks

I especially wish to thank the editors who first published the books and chapbooks from which these poems were chosen: John Travis at Portals Press, Keven Walser and Lorie Jareo at CustomWords, Christine Holbert at Lost Horse Press, Kimberly Verhines at Stephen F. Austin State University Press, Hilda Raz and Elise McHugh at the University of New Mexico Press, Victor DiSuvero at Pennywhistle Press, Richard and Pam Brobst at Anabiosis Press, Darby Penny and Ken Denberg at Snail's Pace Press, and Dan Nowak at Imaginary Friend Press. Also thanks to Emily Wendell and Donna Shear at the University of Nebraska Press.

Thanks also to the many friends who have been part of the writing and living communities that have helped me in so many ways for so many years, especially Julie Kane, Art Stringer, Ken Fontenot, Ed Falco, and Steve Gibson, who advised me on this collection.

UNHOLY HEART

From *The Women at the Well*

Eve Recollecting the Garden

Was it your nakedness
or the knack you had

for naming I learned
to love? *Crow*, you whispered

and wings flapped black
as satin in the sky.

Bee, and sweetness thickened
on my tongue. *Lion*

and something roared beneath
the ribs you claimed

you'd sacrificed. Our first quarrel
arose about the beast

I thought deserved a nobler tag
than *Dog*. And *Orchid*—

a sound more delicate. Admit it!
Dolphin, Starling, Antelope

were syllables you stole
from me, and you

were the one who swore
we'd have to taste those blood

red globes of fruit
before we'd find the right word
for that god-forsaken tree.

Noah's Wife Addresses the Department of the Interior

Birds, though they sing
sweetly, can be hell
when cramped in cages.

Cats of all kinds
do not take well to boats.

All primates stink,
albeit they are clever.
Giraffes are a pain
in the neck to feed.
Try it once, you'll see.

Chickens are dumb
and geese are mean.
Swans are not always graceful.

Bears are loners. Wolves
stick with their kind,
though elephants warm up
to strangers rather fast.

The snakes weren't half
as bad as I'd imagined.
Rats—though they, too, have
their place—most decidedly were.

The insects I got used to,
though at first I forgot
and swatted a few. Lizards
are more temperamental

than turtles. Pigs make better
housemates than gazelles.

Now that we just have
a dog and a couple of goldfish,
the place seems kind of empty.
There's too little to pet.

Of the whole menagerie,
I'd say I miss the zebras most.
One dove still comes back
every spring, though
considering the state
of affairs these days,
he is often a bit depressed.

When I think of what we
went through trying to keep
that whole damned zoo afloat—
the times I sat up all night
with a homesick horse, the time
all the deer and elk came
down with the croup . . .

Of course, when the rainbow
arced new hope on the horizon,
I thought it had all been worthwhile.

But I have watched the world
being malled, the waters
fouled, the air clouded
with *progress*, and gentlemen,

if I wasn't a God-fearing woman,
I swear, some days
I'd start praying for rain.

Lot's Daughters Bent on Revenge

He would have given us up
for strangers—his own flesh
and blood—sacrificed

our prized innocence to insure
their safety in his home.
He said it was a matter of honor.

What manner of god rewards
such lack of feeling?
Not once did we see him

hesitate or weep for the lost,
yet she who glanced back
was punished, remains

a monument to pity, captive
of a gesture of the heart.
Knowing his love

of wine, tonight we serve him
into a stupor, then put
him into service—a pleasure

divorced from lust. We know this man
whose love we've never known.
And fuck his honor.

With our sons, his sons, our brothers,
we return like deer
to lick our mother's salt.

Ruth: On Wandering. On Wonder.

For years I listened
to her reconstruct
her homeland in story.
As she spoke, the blue
of sky there turned
sapphire, the yellow
of wheat turned gold.
The scent of fresh baked
bread that filled the houses
of her people filled me
with a hunger—and no eating
could stop the pangs.
The laughter of friends
I knew—though never having
met them—drew me to the center
of a village in my dreams.

I didn't know then how longing
transforms landscape,
how memory can revise a place
we think beyond our reach.
So when she said she would
go back, I said at once
I would go with her.

Loyalty had little to do with it.
Love? Perhaps a bit more.
But my husband was dead and I had been
long gone from my own mother's house.

It was my chance to see the world
made wider, to become part of a story
much larger than my own.

In the book, they stress the leaving
and arriving, but it's the memory
of the journey I treasure
most of all: how spectacular
a sunrise looked above a strange
horizon, how the flavor of the common
food we devoured was enhanced
by the open air, how doggedly
a mule plods on, how in your sleep
you can still ride its rhythm,
how the lilt in a foreigner's
voice brings new meaning
to the simplest *good day*.

Things turn out as they must,
I suppose. The strange becomes
familiar. What I once called home
today seems strange.
I rarely look backwards,
or try to recapture what I left behind
in words, but now that Naomi
is gone, I sometimes wander alone
by the edge of the sea and try
to imagine where all that water
comes from and goes, and where
it might take me if I insisted
on following once more.

Judith Dreaming of Her General

It's a truly grizzly business:
beheading a man. A labor
no training can prepare you
to accomplish and no triumph
can erase from your memory
once performed. I know both

what I saved and lost,
have heard many singing
my praises, but nothing drowns
out the echo of a blade
hitting bone, the cry of terror
sliced into silence. What I did

was necessary, even inspired.
There was a town at stake, a power
beyond my own forcing my hand.
But it was—it is—*my hands*
that bear the weight of the trophy.
That symbol of defeat I cannot lose.

A dozen times a day, I bathe.
I change my clothes compulsively.
Still in sleep I am spattered
in scarlet and smell vaguely
of decay. Then there's his eyes
which I see everywhere, questioning

more than they accuse. At times
they appear filled with longing,

some passion I'm afraid might
be my own. I have heard some pagan
tribes devour the hearts of the enemy
when they kill. In my case
I fear the enemy is eating mine.
I drink myself half sick
most evenings, trying to drown
his face in wine, but it rises
to the surface of every dream
I drift away on, stares out

of every mirror, every well
I peer into, hoping to catch
a glimpse of the heroine
I know I am—the woman who tricked
a general into losing his head,
who pays a heavy price for peace
and knows herself a weapon.

Mary Recalling Bethlehem

Among oxen and asses
I labored. Brought my child
to breath through blood

and pain. I had to cut
his cord myself with one
of Joseph's carving knives,

the one he used
to hollow wooden bowls.
That night I was in no mood

for visitors, but what a flock
of them I got! Strangers.
Some in rags bearing lambs,

others in silks with treasures
and sweet herbs. All following
a light in the night sky

I, myself, had barely noticed,
though I once knew a woman
in Nazareth who read her days

by the movement of stars.
The child was adorable—
like any newborn. I posed him

for his guests on the straw—
still wet, a bit sticky from the womb,
yet resplendent in his swaddling

bands with that little shock
of coal black hair—much like Joseph's,
who acted more the father

than he was, opening his heart
to this strange son he vowed to call
his own to any man who asked.

Anne: On the Darkness in Daughters

About angels I knew nothing,
having seen only a stream of light
that seemed to shine from no source,
having felt only a breeze
that moved no curtain. Just that.
And then my daughter bowing
to a word I couldn't hear.

Mary had always been such
a polite girl, willing
to do as she was told. Although
she did tend to walk with
her head at a tilt, as if she were
keeping an ear cocked to the sky.

After her announcement, she grew
secretive and headstrong,
less docile, yet more resigned.
She developed a terror
of pigeons, yet once I caught her
standing like a statue in the garden
with a black snake coiled around her ankle.
She was admiring it like a jewel.

Poor Joseph! He worshipped the ground
she walked on, but I think sometimes he felt
a little used. And although she was
a decent mother in her own way, she remained
somehow removed from the child.
It was I who often rocked him

when he was fretful with fever.
I who changed him, told him stories
of our people and our past.

I had no earthly chance to see him
grow to man *or* god, so though I died
professing faith, I must confess
to doubt as well. I wanted to believe
my daughter virginal and chosen, but
like any mother who knows the ways
of this world, I sometimes shook
my head and wondered what in heaven's name
could have possibly gotten into that girl?

Salome: The Choreography of Guilt

Shouldn't a good child obey
her mother? Fulfill her
fondest wishes even when
the outcome is blood?

I knew nothing of John
beyond rumors of a man—
maybe mad, maybe holy,
dressed in badly cured hides
and eating bugs. For some reason
my uncle Herod was obsessed—
with both John *and* me—beyond
the point my mother saw as fitting.
She had seen that look before
in my own father's eyes, watched him
shadowing me about the house.

The Baptist didn't know
the half of it. My mother had more
than her reputation to protect.
She had me, and a position
of safety she'd secured for us
the only way she could.
She was a queen. And as queen
she gave me orders.

And I did only what I was told.
A simple dance that raced
the heartbeat of a king.

I did it well enough to earn
the trophy I was granted, though
really, I could never call it mine.

It was *her* desire I satisfied
with my infamous performance.
Her desire to take the head
of the man who had condemned her
and hold it, like a sick child,
in her bloody, royal arms.

The Prodigal Daughter's Girl

She can't imagine I was ever young
and longed for all-night parties,
travel, boys. She tells me
times have changed. I say *not much,*
and insist on her propriety, though
I know she thinks I'm mean
and hates my caring. Perhaps I have
protected her too long, shielded her
too thoroughly from the tongues
that clucked bad omens at her birth.
How can she understand the haunting
of my father's eyes, how they clouded
with shame when I returned to his door,
back from a year's adventure.
My wild oats following me home.

I can still see him scanning the street
for nosey neighbors while I, faint
and famished, though big as a house,
clutched his unforgiving hand. My mother
fed me warm milk and bread, and tended
me with kindness, but she hid her face
in her veils when she walked through
the village, until the day she ran
bareheaded, yelling for the midwife,
who scowled at my pains and left
abruptly when her work was done, saying
another girl, as she gathered her coins.

She asks me very little of her father,
perhaps knowing, despite her innocence,
that I have little beyond passion
to tell of. Still, I think she seeks him out
in the eyes of every gangly boy who sings
to her sweetly or offers to help her
fetch water home from the well.
The stark pleasure of her smile
confirms my worst fears. Yet how long
can I keep her from feeling what she will—
what I once felt myself? I pray
she may be right about the times.

But in the town that has sprung up
around our village, I see too many
women wandering in rags, their few
possessions stuffed in sacks and wagons.
Some talk to themselves in low
conspiring voices, some scream endless
curses at the sky, some huddle in doorways—
silent, nursing bottles of cheap port
or their own aching arms. They look so familiar
they frighten me into blindness.
I step past them as if they were shadows
that will disappear with the sun.

My daughter once called one a pig—
the only time I ever slapped her.
She ran away then for three days
I spent terrified—regretful and sleepless.
When she came back, I wept
into her hair like a baby. I fixed her
roast veal, her favorite meal, and opened
a good bottle of wine. Drunk that night,
like giddy sisters, we laughed
and raised our cups to a summer moon

that rose full and circled by a faint
blue haze. Its light touched something
in both of us, igniting dreams
we share but need to keep to ourselves.

Since then, I let her stay out as late
as she wishes, trusting what is free
to leave will most often welcome returning.

Pilate's Wife Welcoming Nightmare

I dread my husband's hands
on me these days, the rough palms
and gnarled fingers raw
from so much scrubbing—
as if he could be so easily
cleansed of guilt. He knows
not even what he does. Or why.

I refrain from saying
I told you so, but didn't I
warn him of the troubled dreams
I saw at once were omens:
first, three green birds
rising toward a black sun, then
seven red roses melting in a stream,

and finally, myself in white
upon a desolate hillside, spreading
my arms as if about to fly—
when, suddenly, that silent Jew
he had scourged to please
the crowd that day was there
with me. He nodded. Waved me on.

I knew not what these visions meant,
but I knew they must
mean something—some *thing*
here was simply too great to ignore.
But ignore my husband did. Laughing

my intuition off as moodiness
or indigestion. He prides himself

on being calm and cunning, just
as he prides himself on cleanliness—
not seeing that obsession lies
behind his newfound urge to wring
his hands like so much sopping cloth.
I love him still, but can no longer
bear his touch, having dreamed

his flesh these past three nights
fallen from his bones. His skull
leers much too close behind

the lips he tries to press
to mine, and my desire is quenched
by a weariness that puts out
fire far quicker than the water

he plunges his arms into night
after night. I think it's blood
he still feels on his hands.
I close my eyes, hoping to find
that stranger on the hill again.
This time, I will let the dark winds
take me. And I don't care where I land.

Martha to Mary: The Quotidian Demands of the Flesh

I remember well when Jesus
said we do not live
by bread alone, but I *don't*
think he was telling us
we need not ever cook.

If the body is to rise,
it must be nourished.
If it's to be nourished
well, it must be fed.

And once we eat,
there are plates that must
be washed clean. To wash them
water must be fetched from wells.

To bake the bread
there's flour, which must
be sifted. Seeds must be
planted to grow wheat
for flour. And food leaves
crumbs, which must be brushed
from tables, or there will be
mice who will scatter
those crumbs on floors.

Don't think I never
felt the urge to hang up
my apron and join
the men who sip wine

while we serve them, debating
scripture while we're out
dressing lambs.

But if we don't, tell me
who on earth *will* do it—
the never-ending work
that must get done.

Fires burn out.
Clothes rip and must
be mended. Milk spoils and
carpets do not clean themselves.

I work my fingers
to the bone and never
get a thank you. A little
help from you, it wouldn't hurt!

The lilies of the field
are fine, and dust to dust
is poetic, but sister, what
we've got here is just plain dirt.

Mary to Martha: The Theological Insignificance of Dust

Why fret your white-gloved
fingers soiled with what
we'll *both* someday become?

Smash the dishes.
Melt the copper.
Let the fabric of our tunics
rot with sweat.

Let the garden go
to weeds, which after all,
are only flowers that persist
without our planting.

If our guests want bread,
direct them to the kneading.
If they want wine, then
let them fill the jugs.

Don't burden me
with details or fault
my desire to sit at the side
of the man who opened
our own brother's grave
and bid one on his way
to dust to rise and return
to the untidy world he loved.

Mary Magdalene's Chapter and Verse

It may have been more
than mere irony that
what some call a *fallen woman*
was the first allowed
to see a risen god.

I had known seven devils
and enough men to recognize
pure spirit when it came
to me, though for a moment
even his mother was
reluctant to let her
virgin heart rejoice.

And those eleven so-called
chosen few—they wrestled doubt
till they could lay
their hands on his skin.
It took open wounds to convince them.
It took the sight of blood.

I have never let them forget
their hesitation, because
I believe our master
left a message for us here.

I think his stay among us
made him feel passion
has its place in Paradise.
Perhaps, like me, he realized desire
is not so very far from faith.

Some men, after all these years,
still want to stone my tainted past,
but I heave them back
the rock of their disbelief
and ask whose load drags
heavier into heaven.

They have yet to find
an answer they can live with,
so they hand me the oldest lines
in the book. I laugh them off.
If you ask me, their apple
story is mostly sour grapes.

I know they wish they had been there
for that first *Hallelujah!*
To witness the radiance
that filled the tomb
as I have described it
again and again, so they will
always remember how
this fallen woman, who once cradled
his cold, human flesh
in her arms, in that moment
rose above them, with a glimmer
of light they dream of
seeing hereafter, held now
and forever in her
dark sinner's eyes.

Mary: A Confession and Complaint

Legend shows me acquiescent.
Don't believe a word. I would have ignored
that angel if I could have, but he made me
an offer I couldn't refuse.
Even now I blame my failing vision
on those few moments of terrifying light.

I was not an ambitious girl.
I loved Joseph and looked forward
to our marriage and children who would grow,
and in their time, have children.
Our days, I assumed, would be simple.
Joseph in his shop. Me in my kitchen.
At night we'd share the better moments.
I would shine beneath his
hands like polished wood.

It wasn't fair to ask me to bear all that
pain without ever knowing pleasure.
And if I could have only one child,
I would have much preferred a girl.
My son, though I know he loved us,
was never affectionate. He moved
as if his body were not his own.
He had a cold, distant look in his eyes.

And Joseph, though he was always kind
and never doubted me, could not get close
to the boy. He grew more silent
with the years, more sullen.

And I could never bring myself to say
forget about the angel! Or to confess
the desire he might have found in me
if he had dared to look
beyond the piety, beneath the veils.

The Women at the Well

We enter on cue, bearing
prophecy, earthen vessels
waiting to be filled, directions
to the homes of fathers, brothers,
husbands who always take
you in and treat you well.

And we are taken in by your telling:
Tales of how one learns to walk
in a foreign land, moments past
recalled by one who never watched
them happen, plots still being
written in which we wait
for our names to appear.

We hear most when we are least
observed, so we are often silent,
serving the choicest meats
from our larders, the saltiest
olives, sweetest breads, red wines
from deep in our cellars, where we
carefully rinse the bottles clear of dust.

We always fill your cup before
it is quite empty. We have learned
how to keep strangers talking,
our own thirsts quenched.

This is what keeps us returning
each day to the circle of women
drawing buckets from the circle
of stone at the center of town.

We soak clothing, refresh weary
livestock, wet our lips, composing
our own stories as we wait
for our reflections in the mirror
of water to speak
what we have always known.

From *Retreats & Recognitions*

Note from the Imaginary Daughter

I have no daughter. I desire none.
WELDON KEES

Mother always swore your plunge was faked
so you could vanish—unknown—into travel.
I waited for a postcard—some sign I could take
as proof she was right. Some thread I'd unravel
back to you—wherever you were. Mexico,
she guessed.
    In pictures you look sad but kind.
Mother said you were brilliant but confused.
She said I might not like the man I'd find—
if I ever did.
    She said you'd only used
her love for art; still she wished you'd let her go
along.
    She kept the poems. The paintings, too.
And I composed myself a father who
filled my desire—a man too real to mourn.
Some nights I dream you dead. Some days, unborn.

Norma Jean Dreams a Blonde Finale

First thing I recall is my mama gone
mad, hurt too hard to care about me.
Or anything. She disappeared
like my daddy, like sunlight before
a sudden storm. Left me a succession
of loveless women. Worse men.

When I discovered my own body
was a way out, I took it. Left behind
my name, my pigtails, cheap
hand-me-downs worn, like patience,
thin, bursting at the seams.

Distance lets you recreate
who you are, where you came from.
Bleach your hair and bat your eyes, whisper
like your breath's not quite your own
and it'll drive some grown men gaga.
Anyone who knocks my acting
has never seen me when I'm not.

Stacked, they call me. *Bombshell*.
Something pretty that's set to explode.

A Little Like Dorothy

It's the story of America's small towns.
So many who called them home once, leave
because we think these towns will never change.
We fear the familiar routines, dull jobs, the same
small minds too dulled by routine to dream.
So we escape, vowing never to return.

But *home* is a word that demands return.
Despite ourselves, we head back to that town
from time to time—if not in real life, in dreams.
And for years it feels like we have never left,
like no one leaves. Everything's the same:
the cop giving tickets, the clerks giving change,

same mayor, same mailman, same women in their yards
   exchanging
gossip and recipes, kids still taking returnable
bottles back to the store for spare change—it's all the same
as when we left, as if time had been suspended in that town—
so no one ever changes or dies. Even the leaves
cling to the trees long past Fall, and the dream-

homes people mortgaged more adventurous dreams
to own are preserved like relics, as immune to change
as the people themselves, who rake and burn their leaves
each Fall, plant the same annuals when Spring returns,
as it always does, just as we do, to the towns
we left, counting on them always being the same.

But one day we notice things are *not* the same.
At first we feel like we're moving through a dream,

but it's real all right—that missing church, the town
houses where a field once bloomed, the store that's changed
into a *shoppe*, the NO TURN sign where we've turned
our whole lives, the factory laying off or granting leaves

of absence more permanent than ours. These changes leave
us feeling out of place. We mourn the same
places we cursed and fled, and wish we could turn
back the clocks, preserve the towns as they appear in our dreams,
where they're peaceful, familiar places, a welcome change
from the suburban sprawl that's ruined so many small towns.

America's changed and left us feeling lost
in a geography of dream towns—all the same.
They call us home. They leave us. We return.

Retreat

The novices led us
in prayer and solemn novenas.
Their silence and black habits
trailed the cloister's corridors.

But we were tired of the protection
of Our Lady of Hungary, and took off
with the Saint Joe's crowd,
who taught us how to inhale

Lucky Strikes, shake
aspirins into cokes for a buzz.
A senior from Perpetual Help
explained to us what *fuck* meant,

diagraming the details
on the back of her missal
during a morning High Mass.
I daydreamed through

the Offertory and the Consecration,
wanting to witness the miracle
of a boy's body doing
what I now knew men did.

When the bells chimed I lined up
for Communion with the other girls,
though the sin I had in mind
was surely mortal. I crossed

myself as the priest
whispered *Body of Christ.*
In my unholy heart, I knew
there was no turning back.

Modern Clothing

Bent over Singers like saints
before altars, half the women
I knew sat, row after row, stitching
the pockets, inseams, cuffs, and flies
of men's dress trousers and boys'
sports slacks. For forty hours a week
at *Modern Clothing* they labored themselves
into eyestrain and bad backs.
Now and then, one of them—
rushed into carelessness—would sew
through her own skin, the relentless machine
piercing three or four times
before her foot winced off the pedal
and the needle, stippled red, came to rest
against her finger bone, drab threads
imbedded in her flesh like a crude tattoo.

Piece Work, they called it. And for years
I saw my future there, hunched like my grandmother,
who worked waistbands and hauled home
bags of fabric scraps she stacked
in closets and corners. Having forgotten
what she was saving for, she continued,
for decades, to save—until the room
we were forced to share left little room
for us, and I developed a need
for space, the urge to discard.

I despised every square inch of cloth
she found a use for: the mismatched

slipcovers and pillowcases, doll clothes
of severe navy serge, the piecemeal wardrobe
she persisted in wearing despite
drawers full of better dresses
she was saving *for good*—an occasion
I realized early on would never be
good enough for her to squander
on something store-bought, not made by her hands.

She died with her hoard still piling up—
a stash of stuff we deemed useless,
carted off to Goodwill, where today I am
searching for a bargain, hoping to find
something *vintage* perhaps, a garment
that has survived long enough to come back
into fashion, a remnant from a stranger's life
I can salvage and put to good use.

Theadosia Comes to the New World

As we drove toward the docks
in the cold before dawn
my mother fingered her rosary beads,
whispering my name as if
I were already gone.

Before I boarded, we embraced
in silence, and I tried
to brand the image of her face
in my mind, knowing this was the last
we'd ever see of each other.

Then I watched from the deck
as my past receded into a blur
of lights, and there was nothing
left to see but a slow sun
trying to burn through the fog.
Gray sky seamed to gray water.

Each day I'd sleep through
the warm afternoons, then pace night
after night along the cold steel railings,
trying to conjure my husband's face.
He'd sent no pictures,
saying, *Think of the cost.*

I had no idea
was he tall or short?
What color was his hair?
Would there be any kindness in his eyes?

He'd written only of a farm,
how hard he'd worked to save
for my passage, how soon
we would work together, and perhaps
save enough for a cow.

I never noticed I was being watched
till one evening a man stepped up
behind me. He said *Orion*
and pointed, thinking I watched the stars.
From that night on, I did.
He taught me to plot
our direction by their light.

Don't ask me what love is.
Sometimes the heart finds what it needs.
I married a man I met between
two worlds, held him like a part
of what I'd been and was no more.
The man who had sent for me
was offered a sister—who was stronger,
more loyal, able to work twice as hard.

When that boat docked, I was the first
to disembark, carrying my suitcase
of practical clothes, and inside me,
already, my American child.

Plot Lines

Each day she rises, and each day's a tale
that tells her what it is a life entails.

She questions purpose, chases meaning
round and round, like a dog on its own tail.

The best of times can be the worst. One city like two.
We learned the truth of that from Dickens's tale.

God, if she exists, didn't create us only
for work and worship. She loves our small human details.

Saints from sinners, lovers from lust. Enemies
befriended. *How so's* the never-ending human tale.

Two red birds in tall brown grass. Grackles in the maple.
One crazed squirrel rants. Sashays his silly tail.

The world is made of stories, not of atoms.
Muriel told us that, and lived to tell more tales.

Some days you set out to conquer the world,
but it conquers you. That's why God made cocktails.

I want my poems to be graceful. Do I fail?
Her reach exceeds her grasp. Oh, that old tale.

Fat Tuesday

This revelry reveals our childish greed.
We fight to catch a strand of plastic beads
and grovel on the ground for cheap tin coins

While Black men, all decked out in crisp white sheets,
light the way for debutantes on floats—
with flambeaux poles balanced against their groins.

A lady on a Royal Street balcony
bares a breast. The crowd applauds her tease.
She exposes more, concealed behind her mask.

Miss Piggy hands a joint to a queen in chains.
Dorothy adjusts a falsie; the scarecrow his brain.
A pregnant nun chugs bourbon from a flask.

All this debauchery leads us into Lent
and guarantees we all feel ready to repent.
Tomorrow, still hungover from this bash,
we'll kneel and have our pagan foreheads crossed with ash.

Second Lining at My Own Jazz Funeral

For Nancy and Everette

There ain't a saint among us
but we go marching in
to July's white heat, armed
with black umbrellas
and bottles of Dixie beer.

The drummer's on a roll
and tries to woo me
with *Amazing Grace*, but I'm
distracted by the sax man
who's wailing for *Li'l Liza Jane*.

When our entourage turns off Oak
to strut toward the batture,
I hesitate, then head back
to the bar, not ready
to say goodbye to that river

that has run through ten years
of my life like a Huck Finn fantod,
or the friends I'm afraid
may forget my face too quickly,
or the lover whose bed
another presence will grace

before I'm even out
of this town, where even the dead

have their parade and their party
and get buried above ground
so the water
won't get to their bones.

Star

Never get a tattoo
more interesting than you are.

RED DEVECCA

Back when only sailors had them,
or bikers or sideshow freaks,
I decided my own face
would be the perfect place
to etch a piece of night sky,
that a twinkle on my cheekbone
was a statement I wanted
to make for others' eyes.

Memory reconstructs the messy
parlor, down behind
the Greyhound Station they tore down
a decade ago. Inside the burly owner
displayed his designs like doilies
on tabletops and walls—a few

on his own knotty biceps:
a crouching tiger, a confederate flag,
a soaring eagle above a fractured heart
scrawled with a woman's name—
Was it Sheila? Or Theresa? Was it Mom?
I can recall dusty storefront windows,
how high I had to get myself to walk in,
how I'd glued on tiny sequins
so he could see what I had in mind.

Today I bless him—though I cursed him
then for refusing to take my money,
thankful as he said I'd be, that he
forced me to save future face.
Though I have admired, even envied,
an *ankh* or rose or filigreed knot
spied on someone else's arm or ankle,
I have come to understand the limits
of purchase, and realize time by now
would have turned my own stellar symbol
into little more than scar.

There is, I suppose, a chance
I would have risen to its occasion,
been inspired to reach higher by such
a glamorous mar, but it's probably
for the best I have remained
as unremarkable as I've managed—
satisfied, for the most part,
with my ordinary laugh lines and
furrowed brow, with just enough crow's feet
to hint at what I have, and haven't, been.

Latter Day Saints

They introduce themselves as *elders*,
these three fresh-faced boys whose knock
has roused me from my bed, but blush
bright red when I say *Grace*,
and extend my hand as if I were the one
who had come to witness or solicit
for The Lord. It is, no doubt, the devil
in me who takes pleasure in
their obvious discomfort and keeps me babbling on
about Buddha, the Goddess, my new deck of Tarot cards.
But hell, it may do them a world of good
to see temptation in a black robe
and sweat socks, sleep still sticky
in the corners of her eyes. I may save them
from a fate worse than the fire and brimstone
they came to warn me about—or at least
from the Doberman chained like Cerberus
to the rickety wrought-iron next door.
Once I took heaven literally myself
and practiced what I'd say to the angel
at the gates when I arrived. I forget now
what words I settled on—something clever
and direct as I recall, that would not sound
like mere excuses for the failures I knew,
even as a child, I would accumulate before
the final trumpet blast when we would rise
from our graves like bad actors in B movies
to shuffle toward the clouds where God,
looking like Charlton Heston before

he sold his soul to the NRA, would sit on his
ethereal throne—scary—but nice enough to let me in.
I want to tell these speechless preachers
I am not beyond belief. Far from it. I refuse to be
agnostic about anything except the events
I see unfold, day to day, before my eyes.
Whether they'd call that sin or salvation,
I don't know, and they're far too anxious now
to escape my tirade to explain.
They back off, just slow enough to stay
within the bounds of politeness, inching away
from my sermon till I am left alone in my pulpit,
mumbling to the welcome mat. As I kneel
to retrieve today's *Journal Star*, the morning sun
glints gold as a halo. And I'll be damned
if I don't claim it as my own.

Extreme Unction

My mother has been struck by the Lord.
Physically, this time. An old crucifix
she'd stored on a closet shelf came crashing
down and whacked her in the head so hard
she said that she saw stars. She bled
only a little, needed no stitches,
just an ice pack and a couple of Aleve.

But a bruise bloomed as testament
in the middle of her forehead, right
at the spot where the priest will thumb
his black ash on her come Wednesday,
where Charlie Manson and his girl apostles
marked themselves like Cain.

My mother's a true believer. Devout enough
to keep a cross and rosary in every room,
roses blessed at the Carmelites framed
atop her bureau, a bottle of miracle water
from Lourdes in her refrigerator door.
Yet she's at home enough in the secular world
to embrace a little sacrilege and laugh
when my brother responds with irreverence:
Jesus, you really got nailed.

Though I tend to believe in some Power
That Be, I'm not sure how to name it,
or if we'll meet A Maker or more Mystery
when we go. The only thing I know
is that we will. Still, I find myself

Thanking God my mother only got nicked
this time. It will not always be so—
for her, for me. Someday we'll face
whatever The Hereafter is. Some sacred
speculations will prove fact, and some confounded.
I'm banking on my open mind to serve me either way.

The cross that clocked her has been in our family
for years. It's wooden, and really a kind of box—
the front of which slides back to reveal
a compartment designed to hold candles
and holy water, the basics one keeps
on hand to anoint the dying. Or the dead.
For this, we are wholly unprepared—
the water dried up years ago,
the candles burned one night
when the lights went out in a storm.

For now, my mother puts it back
on the shelf, higher up
in a safer spot, promising herself
she'll fill it someday soon
with all it was intended to hold.
But my guess is life will
get in the way, as it does with so many
well-laid plans and good intentions, and death,
when it comes, will surprise each of us
like the accident, which, as the saying goes,
was only waiting to happen.

Midlife Heavy Metal

I know I'm not the only woman in the world
who spent her adolescence lusting
to a backbeat and still, in some part of herself
she has grown to deny, can't resist
a big-mouthed bad boy, surly siren
in tight pants who swaggers and snarls
and screams his heart out
in the name of Rock & Roll.

There he is on my TV screen:
older than I am and showing his age
but still strutting what stuff he's got.
He's Heathcliff with a microphone,
a long tall glass of water
spiked with acid and desire,
his hair a black mass
of styling gel and tease,
mouth a severe weather warning,
eyes an invitation to a party
we'll regret if we go to. Or not.

Oh, we know better. Or at least
we know we should. But somewhere deep
inside we still long for all the trouble
he could stir up; we want to hear every lie
we know by now his kind tells.
We want to lie back, strut our own stuff,
and be just a little bit like him—
the bad boy every good girl is inside.

On Finding a Footnote to *Truckin'*

To roll along in an easy, untroubled way.
That's how the fine print defines
the word, and this, my friends,
is the Norton Anthology,
so we know it must be true.

They're explaining Diane Wakoski's line,
keep on truckin', to a world that's gone
three decades beyond the use of such lingo,
the hip talk of my youth grown archaic
while I was too busy struggling to get something said
to notice it getting gone.

I am, after all, of that generation
that *trucked* through the sixties. One of those
boomers who elevated *freak* into a compliment
and turned *party* into a verb. But now
we're long past the age we once thought we could never
trust anyone else beyond, and the Xers
who have taken our place are pierced, tattooed,
and dyed in ways we *freaks* would not have dreamed.

Wakoski's no longer the gun-toting moll
she posed as when I first fell in love
with words. Garcia's joined the *really* dead,
left his assets in litigation between two women
in suits and pearls. Even Mr. Natural has probably revised
his image via hair weaves and liposuction, and most nights
I'm too tired to party past ten.

We might have once called this turn of events
a *bummer*—a word the Norton, to my knowledge,
has yet to pin down for posterity, but meant,
if memory serves me right, the opposite of something
far out or *out of sight*. Oh, those shape-shifters
of language: slang. Ibid. Ibid. Op cit.

And what a long strange trip it's been.

Broke Down Palace

The road of excess leads to the palace of wisdom.
WILLIAM BLAKE

Stop by my place, we'll do a nickel bag,
she says, too strung out to recognize
that it's been more than twenty years,
that I have no idea where her place might be
or how much a nickel bag can hold,
that smack, or whatever they call it these days,
was never, thank God, my thing.

I was more your orange sunshine,
purple haze, black hash kind of girl,
a self-professed Blakean—half-assed, wholly
misinformed, but ardent, nonetheless,
in my dogged pursuit of excess, which
brought me no closer to wisdom but did
get me out of this town I'm back in now,
lost and looking for directions to the home
of an old friend who, unlike her, I want to see.

The room is smoke-filled, sweltering,
still she's buttoned down in long sleeves—
covering her tracks, though she can't
disguise the bruise above her eye—
which I don't mention. I'm only in this dive
to use the phone, but she's a regular
marveling at the luck of the reunion.
We had ourselves some times back in the day,
she says, as the bartender hands me my change.

He nods, proceeds to clear away her glass,
swipes the dirty bar with a dirtier rag.

I head for the pay phone, dial rescue,
and hang on the line too long,
conjuring excuses that will sound sincere.
I know but for some grace beyond my name
I'd likely be here too—strung-out,
dead drunk, and friendly to a fault
with whatever took me back to times
I'd convinced myself were better.

At seventeen the road to ruin looked scenic,
and I'll admit there were some stops
along the way I regret less than
the steady stream of respectable days
I wade through now, less out of my mind
but also less alive to the crazy moments
that we lived for then, on the edge
for love of the danger as much as the view.

The best I can manage now is to buy her a shot,
stick around long enough to sip a cold one
before I leave with a promise so vague
I won't feel guilty when I break it.
Even she knows it's a lie
I'm telling for the sake of the girls
we were in a past so far gone
it feels like someone else's life
we are both still escaping.

Lunacy

For Jim Simmerman

The moon's a melancholy whore.
She'll go down on
any night that's got a sky,
shining like a fingernail pairing
or a silver dime.
You could be living on your own
private island, in a cesspool
or a Circle K, drunk
on stale beer or a fine chardonnay,
listening to Bach or the Butthole Surfers—
she won't discriminate, caressing
one and all with her cold light.

Once I had a boyfriend named Cowboy.
1974. Philadelphia.
I had yet to hear that John Prine song,
but yes, a free ramblin' man he was.
The moon seemed more precious then.
More authentic, you might say.
My half-Persian, Lola, when not scratching
her fleas or the furniture, was out screwing
every Tomcat in town.
As I recall, the Mummers canceled
New Year's that year, because
the wind would have blown them
from South Street, up Broad,
straight into Billy Penn's arms.

That would have been no one's idea
of a good day, though *Honey, a bad day*
depends on your definition.

I can still see the sad sun of hope
breaking through. Our headlights punched out
like stars, cut out like Christmas cookies.
We played like gods with our fingers, and Honey
grew less sweet by the hour, so we knew, even then,
she might, by and by, turn bitter
and fling the bauble moon aside
with slippery words she only half believes.

Oh, *c'est las fucking vie* and *que sera!*
The moon's going to tango
all over her eyes anyway,
like a happy woman
walking the streets all day.

Geography Lessons

For Adam Foote

What's Nebraska? asks Adam,
who is eight and curious
about why I have left the familiar
state we both lived in since
the year he was born. Too wide-eyed
for irony, he studies my face
for an answer, a definition of this
marvelous word I now abide in
but can't yet explain. So I mumble
It's flat and far away, trying
to sum up the difference between
now and the four hours of Blue Ridge
we once drove across to visit.

If I had a map, I'd point
almost dead center, as if abstractions
like that would satisfy a child,
even one who understands directions
a damn sight better than I do,
with my endless circling
of back roads and main streets
trying to find my way back
to places I've just recently been.

He knows distance, I'm sure,
and something of longing—
one of the first lessons anyone learns.
But how do I describe the absence here,

that so many fall in love with?
Which words will allow him to picture
the predominance of sky? I take his *what*
at face value, an honest inquiry
into more than location, and struggle
with the wide space in the language
I am still trying to imagine into place.

From *Beholding Eye*

Portraits of the Rich

One can hardly believe their bearing—
posture so regal, one wants to call it
carriage, though motion is rarely implied.
Their faces, composed to inspire
admiration, refuse to give much away.
No museum is complete without a few.

If they are men, their sternness represents
itself as virtue. They stand poised
with a hand hitched in a vest pocket
or finger a shimmering watch fob
to remind us of the value of their time.
Sometimes they sit behind an expanse
of desk, accoutrements of their industry
displayed against dark backgrounds.

If women, they are most often dressed
in white. If not white, then blue.
Their pale throats adorned with fine gold chains,
delicate lace framing the hands that lie
clasped in their decorous laps.
On occasion, they demure behind a fan.
One can barely imagine them unclothed
or caught in the act of disrobing.

Such exposure is reserved for the poor
wenches who were paid to serve as models
for the Masters, and who now gaze openly
at us, and those who deemed themselves their betters,
from much better paintings, hung here
on the gallery's equal but opposing walls.

Large Bathers

After Cezanne

Only one figure actually appears
to be *in* the water. The rest lounge
on the banks, the curved lines of their limbs
sketched against what blue it takes
to make the eye see air,
just enough gold ocher to dust
their skin the warmth of summer.

The women are, for the most part, faceless.
Their features crudely drawn, bodies
painted the color of sand—if they are
painted at all. Sometimes untouched
canvas is left to represent bare flesh.

                    Midpoint
dead center on the far shore
stands a man washed the color of wheat, fully clothed
beside his wheat-washed pony.

His face, too, is a gap, an absence
of detail we read as visage and longing,
since he, like us, is the voyeur
in this scene, the eye
for whom these bathers are composed.

The village in the distance is hardly more
than a dream, despite the solid cerulean
of its rooftops and spire suggesting
civility and containment, which is what

we come to this painting to step out of
for a moment. We enter this idyll to forget
a world that makes us so self-conscious
of our naked selves, we fear
a sight like this might strike us blind.

Mrs. Eakins's Final Touches

After Susan Macdowell Eakins

First your student, then your wife, then your model.
In becoming these, I slowly had
to unbecome myself. I was transformed
into another of your finely rendered subjects,
a life-like figure you composed in enigmatic light.

Oh, I know you loved me deeply and bragged
to others often that your Susie had an eye
for color finer than your own, but you had a way
of needing that, too often, overwhelmed me.
I defended you from all those fools
who thought your work too bold.

I do miss you, Tom. Your passion, wit. The wild determination
that you brought to life and art—but I must admit this solitude
your sudden passing left me in some days feels like luxury.
The joy of work's a pleasure I denied myself too long.

What I love best, ironically, is painting images of you.
Your face. Your hands. Your body. Which I resurrect
upon my easel now. It took me years, but, dear,
I think I've finally captured your true likeness.

Life-like. Silent. Staring from the shadows
that I paint you in. Thomas, my love,
you taught me. But not everything I know.

Frida Digresses on Red

After Frida Kahlo

Rojo, we say in my language,
which captures more precisely
its vehemence, the violence
and pleasure it catches in the eye.
The word demands we force out
breath—not unlike, say
Jesus, who knew the color well,
who was, perhaps, God's metaphor
for what is *rojo* in us all.

In this painting it draws you
to my shawl, offering
warmth against cool blues,
and yet, a sense of danger.
Here it spatters pain
across the canvas; here it blooms—
tiny *flamboyants* in my hair.
There it flashes in the parrot's wings,
and here it is life itself,
ending before it begins.

How I wanted to beget
that life! What pictures
I could have made for a child!
Not grand, like my love's—
who moves whole walls
with his sermons—but visions
in their own right moving.

Parts of my self scraped
with a palette knife, laid on
thicker than blood.

Rojo! To your ear it may sound
close to a laugh, but there is
nothing funny about it. Not in these
matters of life and death, these paintings
that are more me than mine.

Room in New York

After Edward Hopper

Note how many rectangles and squares:
the window we view the couple through,
the three black lines we read
as shutters, three indistinct pictures
that hang on the flamboyant green walls,
the old black upright she pings upon
with a single index finger.
Note how the red of her dress repeats
the lamp and chair, how the stark white
of his shirt echoes the sheet
of what is meant to represent music—
although it is, most curiously, blank.

It is only the figures themselves
who appear to have nothing in common.
Not just that he is absorbed in his paper—
because who among us has not been
so eager to learn the news of the world
that we've allowed ourselves to get lost
in print. But look
                how she sits at that piano.
Not facing it as someone intent on playing would.
No, she sits as if she meant to face *him*,
but has turned to the keys as an afterthought,
a way to entertain herself while she waits
to catch his eye, as she has ours.

Her pale skin is almost ghostly.

The bow on her shoulder
an odd attempt at adornment
like the dead center doily that protects
the small brown table he's leaning toward from nothing.

I imagine her sounding out middle C,
perhaps hitting a sharp for emphasis.
I imagine the piano itself is hopelessly
out of tune, and that both of them have been
waiting their whole lives for attention—
each other's or anyone's—for a song to take them
somewhere beyond the confines of the space they are in.

But his stocks have gone down or his team
may be up for the pennant, and she has
her club or some project to type for the boss.
The city outside is all menace and promise,
all streetlight and exhaust.
We ourselves could, at any moment,
climb a fire escape, pick a lock, tear down
the brown of that door, and be inside
there with them, like them—beside ourselves,
bored to distraction, without a word to say.

Birthday

After Dorothea Tanning

She seems to be asking something of me,
this bare-breasted woman standing barefoot
in her house made of doors—each one
opalescent and opening onto another,
and another, until coming and going
become more or less the same thing.

She looks unfazed by the options.
Her green gaze focused far-off, beyond
any destination I can envision
outside the frame. The hue of her eyes
is echoed in what appears, at first glance,
to be seaweed draping from her waist,
but on closer inspection reveals
a tangled garland of women's bodies,
contorted like the damned in Rodin's
Gates of Hell. She wears them well,
looks both elegant and disheveled,
festooned in purple, green, and gold
like a refuge from some solitary Carnival.

And then there's the creature at her feet:
lamb-faced, rat-tailed, monkey-clawed
and eagle-winged—an animus caught
between *animosity* and *amour* who looks
as if he has just landed or has, perhaps,
been waiting patiently for her
to give a command. He's a guide

any woman might be tempted to follow herself
if the time were right. And time, I think, may be

what this painting is all about—
if paintings are really *about* anything.
Time, which takes its toll on us and composes
all our entrances and exits. Time, which we must learn
to celebrate even as we watch it pass,
with no answers as to where it might take us,
what doors it might open for us
if we get closer, and then too close to close.

Georgia, at Ninety, Learns to Make a Vessel

After Georgia O'Keeffe

Since that day I wasted
an hour searching
for a tube of blue
to edge a bone,
I have known my years
of making color speak
what I can find
no human words for
had come full circle, back
to a black line on white.

For weeks then, I walked
the Faraway, not sad
exactly, certainly not
in despair, but in wonder
of the solid shapes
I could still discern
in shadows.

It made me think
of Stieglitz, for whom
beauty lay in gradations
of light. He could rave
for days about silver
tones, the clarity of grays.

Finally, I realized my eyes
were not so much *failing*,

simply learning the art
of revision as I had
never understood it before.

My hands always did have
a mind of their own. To see
with them is simply
another lesson in perspective.

I roll and coil and roll
and coil and smooth
away the rough spots,
cup my palms around
the clay till I hear it
sing for a glaze.

And if I fail, the object
is still useful.
It stands filling space
in its beautiful way.
And it pleases me
to fire this earth
that holds both air and water.

The Eye of the Beholder

After Diane Arbus

All human beauty is
an aberration, a mirror
trick drawing us
into itself. Into what is not.

And what is desire? A lack
invented by belief,
a return to the thrill
of the unfamiliar we recognize
in an instant as ourselves.

I know this in sight.
In the click of a shutter
revealing the barely real.
Strip glamour of its thin
veneer and you find something
raw. Elegant. You find the part
in us we're all afraid of
staring straight in the face.

But I can't turn my back
or blink. I feel myself
connecting through captured light
to a darkness that beckons, a darkness
much less frightening than you fear.

My subjects appear calm
because they are. They compose
themselves before my lens

like hallucinations we have
all shared, metaphors that suspend us
between what we want
to be and what we become.

Try to picture yourself
beyond denial. Run your hands
across your average face,
your normal body. And tell me
how you differ from these
miracles that always make you
want to look away.

Descending Nude

After Marcel Duchamp

She'll never shimmer for me
    again as she did
        when I was seven, maybe eight

(old enough to read
    the word *descending*, old
        enough to know *nude*

meant she wasn't wearing
    any clothes) & stood here
        in this very room, calmly watching

as she walked out of the canvas.
    She didn't clank, as I might
        have expected, but rather

sauntered silently into the space
    that had been mine, crossing
        a line I had not known was there.

As I recall, I wasn't at all
    surprised (which seems surprising
        to me now) simply intrigued

by how all those angles &
    a few words could make her
        come alive in what I saw

as the actual world. My mom & dad
    were across the room somewhere
        maybe scratching their heads

over the urinal. My brother sulked
    in a corner, pissed that we'd come here
        instead of the Franklin Institute

down the street, where he longed
    to walk through the heart yet again
        & hear its insistent throb.

I see now I had already chosen art
    above science, though this was years
        before I myself turned to words

or saw the world this way again
    through windowpane. Years before
        my brother began to self-destruct

searching for escape or vision
    & my parents turned gray. Today
        the nude appears armored and static

& though her muted tones of browns
    & golds glow lovely in the light,
        she stays within the confines

of her frame. I see, in fact, she isn't
    a woman at all, but a machine
        designed to disrobe the viewer

an idea intended to change
    forever how we see.

Rrose Sélavy No Longer Sings *La Vie en Rose*

After Duchamp

How many years can a woman pose for a man
in the same bad hat & ratty fur
before the world goes gray before her eyes
and even *la-de-la-de-la-de-la* sounds like the blues?

How many nights can she lie alone while
the avant-garde goes galloping toward the future
on their hobbyhorse? I tell you, my heart may belong
to Dada, but even an alter ego needs l'amour

which is more than a mere word and goes beyond mechanics.
Love—so easy to make, yet more difficult to create
by far than art. That's why some people call
this kind of song a torch. And I keep singing—
la-de-la—to make something burn.

Marcel Meets Georgia at 291

What do you see
    in these skyline lights?

The fragrance of motion
    in a Manhattan night.

And do you sense anything
    in these cliffs? This sky?

I hear you seeing
    through my eyes.

And what do you hear
    in this hue of blue?

Something luminous
    that might be true.

And what of these flowers
    made larger than life?

They bloom like a virgin
    on the verge of wife.

And what in my work
    speaks most to your own?

The bones. The bones.
    The bones. The bones.

Where You've Seen Her

After Cindy Sherman

Perhaps you caught her gazing
    at her image in a mirror, or staring
out a window into a distance you thought
    might be yours. Perhaps you saw yourself
in her eyes.

Perhaps it was in moonlight or starlight
    or the blue haze of a TV screen or
the smoke of a seedy bar where the glow
    from her cigarette gathered the night
around, or perhaps it was in sunlight
    so bright

you had to squint. It hurt
    your eyes. Maybe you've never seen
her at all, or so often you have long
    since forgotten to look, allowing
memory or expectation to make what you think
    she is real.

Perhaps you've brushed by her
    in a subway, at a close-out sale,
in some library where she reached
    for the very book you wanted to read;
or maybe in a dream she cruised by
    in a red

sedan, on a black mare, saying something
    you couldn't quite fit your voice

around but desperately needed to say.
      She could be your mother, your sister,
your favorite or most hated aunt,
      the girl

next door, the one you left
      behind, who got away, the woman too
good or not good enough for you, the one
      who never knew you existed, who's been
waiting for you all her life, the one
      you've been

mistaken for. Perhaps you gave her
      your ring, took her cherry, paid
for her lunch, lent her cab fare
      or lipstick, voted her *Snow Queen*
or *Most Congenial.* You might have
      given her

flowers, advice, or hell,
      a lift to the nearest phone booth,
the time of day. You might have opened
      doors for her, or old wounds,
maybe you held her or wished you could
      hold her

or be her or never had been.
      She is always more or less
than you imagined or would have
      her be. She is the stranger you
always recognize. More than shadow
      less than

substance, not quite yours or her own.
      Since she has never really been there,
you know that she can never
      go away.

Her Search for Great Causes

Undue Sexual Desire—Causes:
Excessive eating of all stimulating foods
such as eggs, meats of all kinds, cheese,
chocolate, tea, coffee and all alcoholic
drinks . . . (novel reading and impure thoughts
are also great causes)

JETHRO KLOSS

The weather doesn't help much.
Humidity lays its sticky hands
on every inch of skin.
Even the slight stir of breeze
comes like hot breath
down her neck.

She lies half nude
before an open window
running her tongue around the rim
of a frosted glass of bourbon.
She eats oysters—raw
with extra Tabasco,
scrapes buttered artichokes
between her perfect white teeth.

Scattered across her rumpled sheets
are D. H. Lawrence, Henry Miller,
Faulkner, a few trashy Gothics.
She has been through the tryst
in the hallway, the corn crib,
that gardener in the grass.

She will wait all of August
for the dark and brooding man.
Perhaps a demon, perhaps a wayward heir.
He will sneak up her
stairs in the moonlight
and make her blood run cold.

Her Great Escape

Romance pulls in
to her driveway in a gray car.
Their hands reach for warmth
across the gear shift
as they talk themselves deeper
into the desire they are
trying to talk themselves out of.

The moon's a white slice
in a black sky, like the moons
that tip their twined fingers,
like the Cheshire cat's
half-assed smile,
like all the cheesy similes
she has heard the moon be like.

She'd hand over her credit cards
if she thought he'd drive her
anywhere but crazy.
Pay for all the gas.
But what he's offering is temperate
as the climate, unreliable as the moon
reflected on the trunk of the old Nova
that's parked down the block.

Smooth as Sam Cooke
singing *You Send Me* on the radio,
she bows out on the last refrain
and leaves what might be
possible, idling in the dark.

For Her Villain

The time that she wastes missing him is hell,
though no one banks a fire that has grown cold.
And so she thinks she'll write this villanelle.

Though forms are frames she doesn't fit in well,
she thinks that forcing pain into a mold
of verse might free her from the hell

of missing him. If only she could tell
the truth from all the lies that have been told
and make sense of it in this villanelle,

her heart might open like a prison cell
and she might be released from the long hold
he's had on her. Not holding him is hell.

She tries to tell herself it's just as well.
That even if love could be bought and sold
it would cost her more than this cheap villanelle.

In this vignette, she plays the helpless Nell
tied to the tracks or stranded in the cold.
And like a dark-eyed demon straight from hell,
he plays the villain. Here's his villanelle.

She Has Days

she walks through wondering
        what it would be like

to be someone, anyone
        other than who she is:
                the woman at the market

wheeling a cart piled
        with Pampers and beer
                the housewife in a blue

plaid dress bending
        over a new bed
                of geraniums, coaxing

color from poor soil
        the hard-hatted woman
                on Main Street behind

the MEN WORKING sign, stopping
        the flow of traffic with a wave
                of her strong, slender hand

the girl crouched on her porch swing
        painting her toenails
                pink—the very image

of concentration. It might
        have something to do
                with choices, but she can't recall

ever having chosen to be
        what she is, where she's at
                at the moment

only choosing to sleep
        late some mornings, to rise
                before dawn others—and even

this seemed more a force
        than choice, something urging
                her into or out of dreams

for no good reason, just to watch
        light play as it will across
                sky, through dust

on windows, choosing to wear
        one dress instead of another
                to turn left on the road

where a doe stands frightened
        transfixed by the lights of her car
                choosing to turn the lights off

and watch her shadow bound
        into a thicket, choosing
                to reply yes or no to a question

without thinking, and then
        having to live with the answer
                and think about why she ever

had to give it. But what does this
        have to do with today, when the sky
                divides itself like a palette into shades

of gray it's hard not to see
        as a projection of her own
                mood, some split inside her

between darkness and another
　　　kind of darkness which lies
　　　　　just the other side of a light

strong enough to blind anyone
　　　who chooses to stare straight
　　　　　into it, squinting at the familiar

figure who wanders toward her
　　　in the market offering a choice
　　　　　piece of fruit, at the nursery

bearing seedlings in a plastic
　　　flat, wearing the sleek blue dress
　　　　　she decided to put on

this morning of her
　　　life on this green earth.

From *Nowhere All At Once*

Nowhere All At Once

And content, for the moment, to be
so far above it all, the Rorschach
of midwestern landscape below you
repeating *square, square, square.*

The world looks different
when you are forced to face it
from such heights and before dawn,
in hours when you're accustomed to being
lost in dreams—that other world
you create to help you make sense of,
to recover from, this world

you now look down on, moving between
destinations—each a place you have
called *home*—meaning, you realize, something
different each time, just as this
no and every place you are now,
this up in the air, is where you always are.

Sight/Seeing

Anything's worth observing
in the right light. In a strange city
every garden blooms a riot of local color,
every public square insists you linger
to admire, and every church entices—
a mystery you can't resist entering.

Not just the palaces, the castles, the museums
guidebooks point out as highlights,
but a simple house becomes *architecture*,
and commuters on their daily rounds
strike you as *picturesque*.

Displacement allows you to be all eye,
immersed in the pleasure of whatever happens
to appear. You scan the streets you've journeyed
miles to walk down, too lost in the unfamiliar
to be anywhere except where you are.
Any corner you turn might offer a glimpse
into the actual, caught in the act of being itself.

That moment is the destination you really seek,
the souvenir you hope will survive the trip home
and let you view the block you live on as it might look
through the eyes of a stranger, your own
ordinary made charming as all that elsewhere,
illuminated by a greater regard.

Great Plains Prayer

Bless us, Oh Lord,
and this our Jell-O. Our corn,
our steaks and kolaches.
Our heat indexes. Our wind chills.
Our sunsets and horizons.
Our endless waves of grain and grass.
Our ancestors who started out
for the coast but stopped half-way.
Our nostalgia for their calico,
their sod, their old homesteads.
Our denial of the meth labs
that have taken their place.
Bless our perseverance.
Our unerring politeness.
Our red state politics
and our white, white bread.
Bless our dubious status
as *tornado alley*, as *flyover zone*
and bless all those who fly over,
as well as those of us who, out of
choice or necessity or inertia—
forgive us, we know not why or what
we've done—but, by God, stayed.

Revenant

It was the walk—half amble, half swagger—
that took me back thirty years to an ordinary morning
on St. Charles, waiting for the streetcar to rattle
me to work and watching from the neutral ground
as you headed into the K&B—and my heart, I swear,
it swelled—a feeling so visceral I imagined
some passerby might see it rising above me
into the live oaks that lined the avenue—
like in those old cartoons where Krazy Kat
gazed at Ignatz, her unrequited longing
an untethered balloon bound, of course, to burst.
I smiled (we're back in today now) at the guy
walking towards me. He nodded. His eyes nowhere
near as blue as yours. And you, my love, remained dead,
even as I turned to watch you—back in my world
for that instant—and walking, again, away.

Against Lawn

The midnight streetlight illuminating
the white of clover assures me

I am right not to manicure
my patch of grass into a dull

carpet of uniform green, but
to allow whatever will to take over.

Somewhere in that lace lies luck,
though I may never stoop

to find it. Three, too, is
an auspicious number. And this seeing

a reminder to avoid too much taming
of what, even here, wants to be wild.

The Bat

I only wanted him out.
But he would not go out.
Not when I opened the windows.
Not when I opened the doors.
Not when I turned
the lights on. Or off.
Not when I waved the towel
or blinked the flashlight.
Tried to coax him toward
the basket, the paper sack.

He careened from room to room—
rather gracefully, I must admit.
Graceful for a rodent—
though, technically, I know
he is *not* a rodent, but up close
he sure as hell looked like one.
Up close and clinging, no less,
to a photo of me in First Communion white,
framed in silver and hanging
on the wall of my study.

How positively Goth, I thought,
as I whacked him as hard as I could
with a broom. Hard enough
to drop him right into a potted palm
where he lay—whether stunned
or mortally wounded, I could not say.
I only knew he was *meep, meep, meeping*
as I rushed him, potted palm and all,

outside to the gutter, where I flipped him
into a storm drain with the help
of a garden trowel.

Did I feel a twinge of guilt?
Well, yes. But mostly I felt triumphant.
Because I had proved myself a woman
who takes care of such things—
and with a minimum of panic. I had screamed
only a couple of times—and then,
not loud enough to wake the neighbors,
who slept on in their darkened houses
beneath a dark and moonless sky.

Next day, that nightmare showed up
on my doorstep—crippled but determined
to survive. I marked his progress
across the walk, into the grass, then out
onto the walk again, dragging
the wing I had mangled all the way.
He rested for an hour or more
beneath a budding peony, and then
he mercifully disappeared—or so I thought.

We all know how pesky absence can be.
How curiously present. Curiosity,
we know, killed the cat, and maybe
killed the bat as well, but still
it has got the best of me. I can't help
wondering where he's gotten to,
or what may have gotten to him.
I keep thinking I see him again
out of the corner of my eye—
though it turns out to be
a fallen branch or a starling
circling overhead, or nothing
at all I keep conjuring back to life.

Of course, I think of the albatross,
the raven—other messengers
turned symbols of remorse.

I only wanted him out.
But he would not go out.
And now, there is a part of me
that can never let him leave.

Gray Ghazal

A day so gray you could mistake it for night.
February: longing for more light.

I try Bach. Big Mama Thorton. A bluegrass reel.
But the savage beast refuses calm. It's hungry for more light.

Phone calls. Snow totals. Eighteen inches. Two full feet.
I should feel lucky—my burden's rather light.

But it's enough to bend *my* shoulders.
I piddle on the piano keys, crack a Corona Light,

think of those nearly dead who return
to tell the living tales of being beckoned by a light.

What do they make of days like today?
Do they regret resurrection? Or make light

of such simple darkness—the mere gray
of weather, the seasonal absence of light

like an absence of grace, a falling down
into darkness. Ah, that! Our human plight.

Our Waitress's Marvelous Legs

It's men I'm prone to eye, but when she comes
to take our order, I'm too distracted
to think beyond drinks, too awed
by the ink that garments her limbs
to consider appetizers, much less entrées.

It's not polite to stare, I know,
but the fact of her invites it.
Why else the filigreed ankles,
those Peter Max planets orbiting her
left shin, that Botticelli angel soaring
just below her right knee?

She's a walking illustration, adorned
to amaze, yet as seemingly nonchalant
as the homely white-sneakered HoJo girl
I myself once was, describing the specials
of the day, listing our options for dressings,
then scribbling the choices we make
on her handheld pad.

My companion can't help wondering how far
up the ante goes, says he bets there's a piercing
or two at the end of the, so to speak, line.
I'm more inclined to ponder motivation
and stamina—how long and how much
she suffered to make herself a work of art.
For I have no doubt she sees her flesh
as a kind of canvas. Her body as frame

and wall and traveling exhibition,
a personal statement on public display.

Same could be said of the purple tights
I wear beneath my frilly black skirt—
too bold a choice for some people's tastes,
but not a permanent commitment.
Clothes make the woman *more*
than the man, despite the familiar adage,
and body as both self and other is
a contradiction we live with, however comfortably—
or not—we grow into our own skins.

I'll admit part of what I feel
is admiration, even envy.
Whatever she may ever become
in this world, she will never again be *drab*.
She'll wear this extravagance
of color and form as she grays
into more—or less—wisdom.

But tonight she simply performs
her duty as server, courteous and efficient
as she does what she can to satisfy
the hunger we walked in with, but not
the hunger the sight of her
demands that we take home.

The Persistent Popularity of Angels

They seem to be everywhere.
Proliferating like rabbits or roaches.
More revered than Jesus or Madonna.
They dangle on earlobes and perch
on receptionist's collars, peer out
of our TV screens and hover
near the top of the Best Sellers' list
amidst diet gurus, vampires, King, and Steele.
They have their own display at Barnes & Noble,
where they've pushed celebrities, politicians,
and one lingering inner child farther back
on the overcrowded racks.
                              I have seen them
stuck to the bumpers of pickups, though
I couldn't get close enough to tell
if they were Seraphim or Cherubs. The latter,
I'd guess, since the latest crop seems heavy
on harps with nary a flaming sword in hand.
More often than not, they're Pre-Raphaelite,
gauzed in ephemeral flesh—though on occasion
they're dressed drab as accountants as they tread
the shaky moral ground we fear won't hold
much longer.
                    With this many celestials
among us, heaven must be damned-near
deserted, FOR RENT signs littering the gold-lined streets,
where God wanders, feeling abandoned.
Meanwhile, down here we're all growing jaded.

The little plastic dolls we've wrestled for years
to keep straight atop our Christmas trees
look gaudy by comparison—like over-made-up
drag queens, who are also, these days, in vogue.

Two for The Bard and Bob Wood

I

Boys will be boys. And boys played all the girls,
who often, in the comedies, appeared disguised as boys
to test the love of other "real" boys—who often loved
other "real" girls (who were, of course, played by boys)
who often did not love them back or loved their money more.
And we think *we're* postmodern, experts in irony,
deconstructing gender—and everything else under the sun.
Read, my friend! You'll see, it's all been done.
And yet, we're apt to do it all again, having learned
neither from history or art. We long for what
we cannot have—the way of madmen and lovers.
It's greener grass on the other side and déjà vu all over.
Desire leads us to lie and lay—and sometimes lie while laying.
That's true for boys, and as for girls—well, that goes without
  saying.

II

The play's the thing and all the world's a stage.
I guess that means we're all just playing parts,
fulfilling roles demanded by the age—
and fate. Our own sweet wills, our aching hearts'
desires, our urges, goals and plans, our instincts—
all fodder for some playwright's scratching pen
which sounds better than *keyboard*, don't ya think?—
though both can do the job of setting scenes
and weaving webs of dialogue between
the characters we all, supposedly, are.

All audiences are tough, directors mean,
and yet, we're all convinced we can be stars.
We learn our lines. We give each act our all.
The curtains rise. And then the curtains fall.

Unrepentant Prayer

Bless me, father, for I have sinned,
my last confession was ten poems ago
and in it I admitted—of my own free will—
how much and how often I have
enjoyed the act of sinning, so much so
no tally of penance is likely to absolve me,
since any promise I make to sin
no more will likely break
down faster than
a two-beat line.

Once the word's made flesh, all hell
breaks loose in babble. We try our best
to *make sense*, but *sensual* is bound
to win much of the time.
That's the inevitable and unholy name
of the game we can never win
for losing, because we didn't
make the rules—and besides—
they are subject to change.

But father, doesn't God—being
omniscient and all—already know that?
So shouldn't he also know
that a repeat performance
is sometimes half the fun?

One perfects one's human imperfections,
seeking out temptations, near occasions
of sin—be they venial, be they mortal—

till the original sin becomes one's
second nature, what you might call
a *calling*—a talent you develop
because it's part of what you are.

So father, let's forget about
contrition, declare unconditional love
for our foibles, our failings,
our inevitable fuck-ups. Now
and at the hour of our deaths, sing
Hallelujah. Glory be.

Off the Map

Wherever you go, there you are the bumper sticker read.
A woman driving the red Explorer that cut right in front of me
on the freeway. As I hit the brakes, I had a vision of where I was
   going.

I wasn't really looking forward to the destination, just going
on autopilot, convinced mere motion was progress of sorts.
   Though I'd read
that being fully present where you are was key, that had never
   worked for me.

I felt restless, vaguely *in*sufficient—wherever I was—a part of me
always longing for something that wasn't there, eager to get
   going while the going
still felt good, to zoom past the mythical crossroad before the
   light turned red.

But now this passing stranger startled me into attention, like a
   siren or a red
light flashing in my rearview mirror. I realized the road ahead
   of me
was nothing but more road, that I had no idea where I was
   going

or why or what I'd do when I got to wherever it was. That I was
   only going
because I didn't know how to stop, spinning my wheels so fast I
   failed to read
all the signs saying *slow down* or *detour* or *exit here*—beckoning me

to pull over, get out, stretch my legs for a while, figure out what
was driving me.

The woman in red was long gone. Perhaps she'd already arrived
where she was going.

And I'm still going strong. Here and there. Another woman.
Another story you've read.

Still Life in Red

The cardinal wasn't much, but it was something.
The *one positive thing every day* she'd vowed
to notice while she could. She watched
him flit from cable wire to lilac bush
to feeder, thought to herself,
this is the very essence of red in flight, and then—
in the next instant—she felt absurd, a little guilty
for thinking so long
about a mere bird.

Shouldn't she be keeping her loved ones
foremost in mind? Her husband?
Her two devoted children?
Her many friends? All of them
struggling to disguise what was already
grief with over-anxious attention.

This was, after all, her death bed.
She knew this, even though they forbid her
to say it—as if not speaking
the words could make the fact of it
less real. It was as real as the cardinal
now perched back on the cable wire—
joined by his less spectacular mate
and singing *pretty, pretty, pretty* . . .

There she was—distracted by birds again.
Did she want those birds to be
the last thing she laid eyes on?

The last thing in—or on—her mind when
the moment—if it was a moment—came?

It dawned on her—*who would know?*—
which made her want to laugh, though
laughter, of late, led to coughing,
led to pain. If someone—
or something—like God exists, as she
still sometimes suspects, would this god care
what final thought carried her over?
What last spot of color filled her
eyes before they closed?

The cardinal, back at the feeder now,
extracts a seed and cracks its shell
in his stout red bill, emits a brief
whoit whoit, and flies away.

Already she sees a summer day scattered
with sunflowers. Blooming without her.
Turning their golden heads toward a golden sun.

Flicker

Fireflies. Their calls to their own kind stuttering the sky with light. Our jars where we thought we could hold on to their magic for a while. Our first small murders unmourned amidst the action: *thwack* of ball on concrete, *frripp* of baseball cards clothes-pinned to Schwinn spokes (those rookies now worth a thousand bucks), rumble of doll carriage carrying Tiny Tears around the block for an evening stroll. The hale of *ready or not, here I come* as you huddle on the street side of your dad's blue Olds, careful to plant the dead giveaway of your red Keds behind one of the whitewall tires he scrubs by hand. From this vantage point, you spy the kid that's *IT* heading towards the silk mill, leaving the telephone pole deemed *Home Free* open for your safe return. And you're about to run for it, to beat, for once, the big kid at his game. But as you round the bumper, you happen to catch a glimpse of a neighbor through a picture window—the crabby old guy who lives alone, always yells at kids to keep off his grass. He is staring at what you know must be his television, at Perry Mason forcing another confession on the stand or one of the season's posse of cowboys reaching for his holster. But from where you are crouched, it looks as though he is staring into space. At nothing. And part of you realizes that, TV or no TV, that nothing is really there. And suddenly traffic, cars, kids—everything pauses. And your throat, for no reason you can name, feels dry. Thick. And you stay there, hiding in something like wonder. Watching. Ignoring the cry of *allee allee in free* as the streetlights flicker on all up and down the block of what, just a moment ago, had been your more or less happy childhood.

Against Prayer

I'm all for praise and gratitude,
wish fulfillment, imagination as act.
And despite a healthy skepticism,
still believe in the possibility
of something bigger than we are.
I'm even willing to call it *divine*.

It's divine *intervention*
I wonder about. Or worse,
the lack thereof, the facile
excuse of *God's will* when
shit happens, as it, inevitably, does:
Unto us. To others.

But if God took the time
to will *you*, let's say,
good looks, perfect health, the yacht
docked on the Cape or in the Hamptons,
but some other poor soul nothing
but deformity, disease, and
a cardboard box in some fetid alley,
what does that say
about God's sense of fair play?

And if, as I heard some true believer proclaim
on Oprah, God sent angels to help her
find her lost wallet, even that perfect
parking spot at the crowded mall,
why then doesn't God
(*for God's sake*, we might ask)

intervene in bigger brouhahas?
Pick a war, a recent fire, flood, or tornado
any disaster or atrocity unfolding
somewhere on earth that sure as hell
deserves heaven's attentions.

Everyone asks *why me?*
But rarely *why not?*
when things get all Job-like,
and we turn to supplication
in the hope of gaining control, pleading:
Lord grant, Lord spare.
Lord, take care of me and mine.

So human of us to see ourselves
at the center of creation,
our own little worlds as *the* world
where God is always on our side.

I say let's leave God
to contemplate the image
we have made him in.
Sing *let it be*, but try
to make what *is* a little better.
Give faith and hope a rest
and concentrate on human charity,
the tender mercy that, soon or late,
all of us need, so let's shut up
and show some. Amen.

Corsons Inlet

After A. R. Ammons

I hike once more this morning, summer easing into fall,
down the path, across the dunes,
        then right, the long way around
                along the shore
                        imagining
I follow your footsteps
though forty years of sprawl has altered the landscape
beyond any route
                I can map
            out of your words—
There are more
straight lines, more blocks and boxes
                than you would have
                encountered,
condos profuse now
            as gulls
on both inlet and ocean side,
                    but nature
still seems to prefer
            the curve, to insist
on meandering
                as your mirroring mind did,
                    as mine does now,
back to your poem, which I have been reading
            each morning, hoping
                it will reveal
                        something

about this place. And poetry.
                    The mutual geographies
            we have explored.
Most afternoons I head to the beach,
        kick off my flip-flops and
                                plunge
            into the waves
                regardless of weather
                determined
to get my fill of ocean while I can.
                    But
            today's crisp air prompted me
        to venture
                    across both bridges, past the bored gaze
                    of the toll taker,
                    the drivers who each took
        a second to return my wave,
the fishermen
                who curiously eye my lack
                of rod and reel—
which would at least give me a reason for being
            out this far
they could understand.
But I amble
                without purpose.
No direction. No goal.
        Destination
                being anywhere
                        I end up.
Could a life be lived as aimlessly?—
            each day a disorder
of passing
                hours
        haphazard as the welter
washed up on this shore?

And would that be to *savor* or *squander?*
        To accept
the becoming
thought, you wrote
                after your own walk,
but how to do so when the mundane
                        muddies every eddy
            beyond meaning?
And how *to keep life*
                when one's own species
seems to choose death over
        and over?
Marsh grass sways
            susurrus
in the steady breeze,
                as the seasonal swarm
        of starlings
                (*that* hasn't changed)
                        wing
their pretty havoc across a cloudless sky,
                a convergence of chaos
                    ordered
in a mass of motion.
In one pond, I startle two snowy egrets,
                in another
        a great blue heron startles me
as does the woman
                a little further on
                    solitary
        as I am, except
for a cell phone,
                    strange shell
            she cradles to her ear.
I have tallied up my sightings
                of gulls, terns, sanderlings, plovers

a few others I searched
though the Field Guide for,
                    attempting
        to name them
                    into a kind of knowledge—
an ordering
                    of a multitude of disorder,
accounting
beyond counting
                which you came to
                            reject—or perhaps
        just give up on, as I finally do
content to just watch
                all those birds
                            winging it
as I walk
            a new, another walk.

From *MEAN/TIME*

A Riff on the Glyph(s)

For Katie Merz

If a picture is worth a thousand words,
what's a word worth?
What kind of word is *worthy*, anyway?
when the writing is literally—though not
literarily—not necessarily—on the wall,
but kind of off-the-wall, this staging
of a page, this eyeing of sound
resounding in silent spectacle—
sphynxified, Lascauxed, encaved
towards, to-words, these bits
of alphabet (you can always bet on
the alpha, though you can't always con an icon).
What doesn't add up can still be more
than the sum of its parts, its phonemes
phoning home like E.T., beyond the crescent
moon of a comma, the black hole of a period
rendered as white space—meaning *fill in*.
Mean NOT meaning *to be unkind*—
but mean/time, as in *during, all the while*.
A bird in the hand is still a thing with feathers
(unless it's Charlie Parker in the background)
and hops. Or hopes. Or bops like an Egyptian.
Even if you can't (like me) draw worth a damn
you can be drawn into. Or on.

Conditional

And if it were only the trees performing their annual striptease.
Only the leaves, brown and brittle, *scritching* against your window;
only you staring out, your hands pressed against the cold glass.
If it were only that, and the lessening light, which fades like a
  dimming spot
on an empty stage, earlier and earlier, day by day, till night
  becomes the norm.
If it were only loss piling up like leaves, like debts that will never
  be paid back,
absences looming larger than the assets of all you own. Or might.
If it were only the ache, your own body revealing its wear, your
  dreams tethered
by the realization that dreams—if they are destinations—are not
  always reached.
If it were not that you imagine and remember, live life halfway
  between anticipation and
aftermath, which is your own ongoing, the *during* you so often
  miss because
you imagine and remember more. If it were not so hard to
  imagine your own demise,
your own un-being in the world as you see it, then you might
  really
see it only and for what it is. And winter would be a metaphor
  for nothing.
And if you had no metaphor—no *this is that*, no *like* or *as*.
If you had no *as if* or *if only*, then what would you make of your-
  self in the world?
Would there even be any making? Would *if* be the only thing lost?
And then? And only? Then.

MEAN/TIME

Desire always looks forward,
craves and anticipates, reflecting
a sky full of menace and promise.
Sometimes longing transforms
a mere glance into gaze.
Intermittent flashes into insight.

*

There's no getting around
all the things you never
got around to doing.
That is the nature
of regret. Now *remorse*—
that is something else entirely.

*

Happenstance
just happens by.

*

Today you will follow
the lure of a line,
tomorrow the seduction
of a sentence
until inkling finds its way
into utterance.

*

It's not as if words
have ever gotten you anywhere—
at least any *where* you could stay.

But still.

But always.

*

Always, in some way, *between*:
time place
dream memory
plans plans plans

meanwhile there's the *time being*
that is (or was) our only life—
which we miss because
we are bent on desire
for more than, other than.

Is this the inevitable
we were born for—
the persistent urge
for becoming more
as we continue to move
toward our unbecoming?

*

Mind a known habit
you can't quite break.
And this, the only world
you live in. And too often ignore.

*

Our hearts full of desire,
full of menace and promise.

But still. But always.
Having the time of your life.

"Books Become Windows"

Look in or out, but refuse
to pun on the word *pane*.

Notice the glass—dusty
or streaked or spotted
by hard splats of rain or—
what's that?
        A slight crack
that spreads like a spider's web
        interrupted
in the spinning.

You have almost forgotten
about reading—the words
mere marks on the page—

so immersed are you
in looking outward, entering
the world they allow you
to inhabit and create
        your own
shadow, a draft
you rush to close
the window against.

Still Life as Oxymoron

There is no such thing in nature
where even the seemingly unmovable
rocks are performing
a slow erasure
into soil, and the bark
of trees teems with a cosmos
of insects who feed on its meat
while roots creep continually
deeper down toward water which
flows beneath earth far less solid
than it feels below our feet
where skin sloughs off cells
with every step, and above us
leaves transform light into color,
rustling branches that twist,
turn, rise beyond gravity's pull
toward a sky where clouds accumulate
and disperse to reveal a sun that caresses
fruit that ripens into the original fruit that,
as the story goes, tempted us
into the world we are now.

Cezanne knew this. So in his paintings
apples dance, pears pulse,
tables tilt on the verge
of tumbling out of the picture plane.
Bottles, bowls, and ginger jars
are set on the edge
of motion, and an eerie pyramid of skulls

mimics his more famous mountain,
poised between becoming and un-
becoming—solid yet ephemeral
as the variety of light in which
he captured it. Or tried.

Torsos

So easy to lose sight of the body,
even when it hangs in naked splendor
here in this dingy storefront
where both the light
and the espresso are too weak
for your tastes. And yet you come
almost daily to be alone amidst
the clutter and clatter
of coffee cups, to situate yourself
among other backs bent over books
and papers and laptops—like the guy
next to you now, typing with two fingers,
intent on his tiny screen
despite the woman's pubic bush
blossoming in pastels, larger than life
just inches above his head. Across the room
another pearly-fleshed nude curls
fetal against a backdrop of black,
her face a blank but for two dots
you take, as you are meant to, for eyes.
And there, a couple collapsed on white,
who look like they are about to do
what couples might feel inclined to when skin
is exposed with such delight. They appear
so unlike the tight-lipped blonde
who sits cross-legged above them,
or the bodies barely formed into bodies
by dabs of gray on the farthest wall, where they look

in danger of escaping from the canvas
into the room where we sit and sip our drinks,
ignoring them and all they reveal about us
sitting here among them on our walls.

The Wandering Dream

You are walking and with each step
the earth moves—not like Hemingway,
but like hell trying to take over,
like water wrestling into waves,
like nothing quite like anything
you have ever walked on before.

In the trees, which appear unmoved
by the whole mess, eyes in pairs
suggest there *must* be faces,
but all you see is what is looking
back at you. All you hear is the slight rustling
that could be nothing but leaves.

And leaving is what you are all about.
Headed somewhere toward or away
from wherever it is you are now.
If only you had more time, better footing,
or maybe—what you really need:
A place to perch. Or wings.

Momentous

Sumptuousness of sun. Climate
as both setting and psyche. The interface
of inner/outer: you in and of.

Explain it to yourself.

Words as bridges. As the chasm
being bridged, as the fall
into the chasm. Hard as rock—
or water from certain heights.

Explain it to anyone.

The mood lightens in light and everyone
longs to be out in it. Heat—before
that, too, becomes burdensome as cold.

Explain the never of now—

The always
too much or not enough
of our longings,
our satisfactions.

Nothing suffices for more
than a moment. So much bother.
And what we make of it.

Against Proof

If a tree falls
in the forest, does it
make a noise?

Ask the deer
who leap through
the underbrush
for answers.

Ask the birds
who checkmate
their alarm
across the sky.

As for language—
it speaks
for itself.

Where's *word*
sans *mouth*?
Mouth sans *mind*?

What we call
silence precedes
and might survive
what we call *us*.

Enough already.
Too much.
Back to that forest.

Soil seed shoot
branch bud leaf.
Add wind.
Add ponder.

Fret

No news is not always good
news, is sometimes just
an agony of anticipation, a limbo
you hang in, waiting so long
to hear that you begin to dread
what you *will* hear, so the nothing
becomes both a blessing and curse,
comfort and torment, an ever-present
possible not-so-good or worse
you can't help preparing for
like some dutiful scout showing off
badges that prove you were prepared.

But what if the emergency never happens?
What if you end up like Noah—cooped-up
with a zoo and all its crap, but surrounded
by nothing but dry land? Oh, the rock!
The hard place! The damned if you do
or don't, the devil and deep blue sea
you are, once again, caught between.

How do you know when to hang on or let go?
What will the voice on the other end say
when the telephone finally rings?

Sad September Song

Begin with sky—autumn blue
then go beyond:
                    imagine
what you never
imagined you would have to:
                    smoke and fire
and that sky full
of Icarus after Icarus
                    too many
to count, to watch
all that falls and
                    refalls, replays
for days we are all in a daze
of disbelief and grief
                    those who have lost
and those who do not know
if or what they have lost
                    and all of us
in the end, something.

Dyslexical

Words, he said, *mean different things*
to you than other people. It was only a meal
you were discussing this time. Indian, to be exact.

The word was *crisp*, and the bone of contention,
so to speak, was *naan*, but he was having none
of it, and you had no words for the distance

even breaking bread could put between the two of you,
the unbuilt bridge of mutual talk you could not
seem to get across. You passed the *raita*

in silence, sipped your chardonnay, and afterward,
as you walked together toward the car, you wanted to point
toward the drama of sunset, draw his attention

to the sky's splendid display so he might, perhaps,
be moved by it, as you were. You might have said
azure or *mauve* or, more simply, *beauty*, but you were afraid

he might not be able—or willing—to see
what you were saying. So you kept the pleasure to yourself—
the gift of a moment you did not give for fear

he would not have received what you intended.
Something else he might have insisted should be
called by a name you might never know.

Caw

On a white picket fence,
three ominous crows, or maybe
they're actually ravens—
as with so much in life,
you're not always sure
exactly what is what,
though when it comes to these
raucous black birds you can
do a fairly good imitation
of their call—so good
they'll often answer back,
which once, in Alaska, caused
your own mother to look at you
as if she were not quite sure
who you were or where you'd come from.
Oh, you have more hidden talents
than she'll ever know—
and you think that's for the best.
Who wants anyone
knowing all their secrets?
Who wants someone watching
every time they preen
their blue-black feathers
and take off.

Means of Transport

At 9th & South you see a sign
that makes you ponder *Utah*—
the word more than the state—
and what it means. You like
the way it occupies your mouth.
Contains a little *Ah!*
as the place may too—

though you once read a poet
who thought *Omaha*
must be magical (*Om! Aha!*)
and you know that's not quite right.

There's no accounting for sound
and sense. Words signify,
but sing as well.
They may be maps,
but the roads they chart
keep changing direction

even as we drive—or walk,
which is what you were doing
at 9th & South on Saturday
when suddenly Utah became
a possible place to be,

though you have never been—
except for in what may pass
for a poem (i.e., this—
a meandering at best
through a state of mind).

You are stringing words
like rosary beads as you pass
Saint Francis Church.

Poem like a prayer, a place
you walk your mind around in.
Winding your way home.

Dusting the Angel

Midafternoon, the cathedral hushed
except for the click of your heels
on the floor's cold, polished stone.
What little light the dingy day provides
illuminates stained glass Madonnas,
saints you can't identify, and the names
of local patrons whose money guaranteed
they'd be commemorated, if not saved.

You wander down what aisles aren't cordoned off
to casual viewers, admiring the craftsmanship
and patience it took to erect an edifice like this,
a century or more in the making. Generations
of the faithful proceeded, confident the work would
someday be completed, though they, like Moses,
might never enter the Promised Land of it alive.

Lights flicker vigils in crimson cups
and post-Mass incense lingers in the air,
haunting you back to a childhood when you worshipped
in pews not unlike the one you stop to rest in now,
more certain, then, of heaven than you were
of the astronauts the nightly news assured you
would be walking, any day now, on the moon.
Absorbed in what's past for a moment, you almost miss
the man kneeling right in front of you—not praying,
but so intent he might as well be, as he works
his way, methodically, down an outstretched wing
with a small dry paintbrush, gently flicking dust
from the grooves of each finely chiseled feather.

The statue's face is smooth, serene, her blank eyes
angled toward the vaulted ceiling, which shimmers
with gold leaf stars on cobalt blue, to remind us
of a heaven that lies beyond visible sky.

You wonder if he believes in it—that tender of angels,
who you dream of days later on the plane flying
homeward, the precise gestures of his hands
as imprinted in your mind as the paintings
you fought your way through crowds to gaze at,
marveling at what the artists had brought to life
on canvas, brushstroke by brushstroke, some communion
between imagination and act, hand and eye,
evolving into each *masterpiece* you viewed
with a reverence that seemed its due.

Aloft and hovering now between continents,
between time zones, observation and aftermath—
where you are seems as ethereal as our grasp
of *eternal*, yet you know it's as real as that man
in his khakis and gray cardigan, maintaining
the sacred by performing the mundane. Perhaps
he sees his task as a ritual of devotion, or could it be,
for him, a job like any other—what he does
to *earn a living*, as we all must in this world?

Outside the smudged square of your window, a rising sun
gently reddens the horizon, glints off the wing
of the jet that is carrying you back to your own ordinary—
a list of obligations already adding up in your head,
all those *to-dos* clamoring so loudly for attention
they drown out the call to work that feels
more worth your while, the necessary angel
that might ground you in the act of doing,
and make time matter. Or fly.

Glimpse

The world seems to pause
long enough for you to see
you are in it and alive.

Nothing happens beyond
what is happening and
the sheer *is* of yourself

and everything takes hold,
only, in the next moment,
to let go again. And then.

It's as if a door closes.
Then ceases to be a door.

New Poems

Fado

Saudade, the singer calls it—
a kind of longing she claims
lives deep in the Portuguese soul,
and *soul* is what I hear
in the music, without understanding
a word, a sense of nostalgia
I often feel myself. For what?

I do not know, having never not felt it—
a being-on-the-edge-of-sadness that descends
sometimes like mist on even the sunniest day.
Like the blues, I suspect it is akin to passion.
Not depression—something finer,
possessing its own kind of beauty,
a hint of shimmer, like the silver threads
woven into the black dress the singer wears.

She raises her right hand, touches
index finger to thumb, her left hand
to her heart, tosses back her auburn hair
as she stares off into a distance that lies
beyond the audience, the room, the city,
the Tagus, the sea—all embraced in the lament
she wails for what I can only imagine. And do.

Terminal Grief

Even sorrow gets lost in this crowd of strangers
hurrying toward their designated gates—
all of us hoping to make our own on-time departures
despite so many flights being delayed.

A voice over the intercom garbles information,
while the talking heads on Fox blather
their version of news I can't be bothered with,
my own breaking story rendering the rest
of the world irrelevant for now.

The baggage I drag behind me feels impossibly
heavy, hastily packed with what will turn out to be
the wrong clothes for the weather when I arrive—
too late for my father to say *welcome home*, or me to say goodbye.

Sustenance

For months we saw every bite he ate
as a triumph, evidence some fight
was still left in him, some desire
for living—or, at least, for ice cream,
hot dogs, pierogies, chocolate milk.

We kept a running tally of intake,
spoke of calories and hydration,
catered to any cravings he mentioned—
peanut brittle, chicken pot pie, Snickers,
the *pogachels* I learned to make one afternoon
when he said he had a hankering for them,
hoping a familiar taste might bring back
memories of his childhood. Or ours.

We held on as long as we could
to the fiction of appetite, the hope
that we could put some fat back on
his ninety-year-old bones. One day—
half a sandwich, soup, some cake.
The next, nothing but *Boost* or *Ensure*.
Eventually, it came down to broth and water.
Communion bread. Just water.
Then—his final feast of air.

Provisions for the Journey

I wanted to slap that priest
in his fat face when he said
I know it's hard, after hurrying
through my father's last rites.

I wanted to tell him *you don't know shit!*
as he waddled down the stairs,
complaining about how narrow
they were for his size 12 feet.

Not to mention your triple X gut
I thought, convinced he was
more concerned with his late lunch
than my father's final days.
Though it turned out to be several weeks
before his body gave in to spirit.

I kept my anger to myself,
because the ritual—however rushed—
seemed to have brought some comfort.
He slept soundly for an hour, then
called me to his side to make
what I thought might be his last request:

*Get a glass   a **nice** glass.*
His voice was thin, but emphatic.

Put in   three ice cubes   he paused
held up three fingers—as if he were making a pledge
or bestowing a blessing

then   he cleared his throat   another pause

then   *fill it*   *with*   *whiskey.*

And like the servant of the Lord
I tried to be in those long final days,
I delivered that cup unto him.

Prayer

I didn't think it would last this long
he said—surprised at the time
it was taking to get the tedious
work of dying done.

His heart was weak, but persisted
in prolonging itself beyond
what his spirit wanted. His world
reduced to a room furnished mostly
with pills and pain, our sad ministrations.

He seemed to have no fear
of death, confident he had done
pretty good in this life, had earned
a hereafter he believed in.

Waiting became a full-time
occupation, a vigil we, like him,
were forced to keep.

Just too damn long, he said again.
And again. So when he asked us to ask God
to let it be over, we balked at first.
But, in the end, we did.

Father, Faltering

I can picture it still—the first time I saw him fall.
He got so excited when I walked through the door,
he jumped up from his chair, teetered, hit the wall.

The collapse looked so dramatic because he was so tall.
I ran to catch him before he hit the floor,
but he caught himself, straightened up, laughed off the fall.

Other stumbles followed. I didn't see them all,
but heard reports. Each one concerned me more
than the last. I feared one day he'd hit the wall

or floor or chair—his head—too hard. The pity of it all
was how strong he'd always been—before
the stroke stole his balance, increased the risk he'd fall.

Some days he'd struggle down the stairs or inch down the hall
from bed to bath—each journey a slow, painful chore.
A cane in one hand, his other shoulder against the wall.

Sometimes he whimpered like a wounded animal—
though in his prime, he could bellow. He could roar.
A lion may rule his pride, but the mighty do fall.

Near the end, he couldn't walk at all.
He mostly slept, exhausted to the core.
Above his bed, a crucifix hung on the wall,

though he no longer had the wherewithal
to pray for the heaven he had prepared himself for.
We waited, breathless, for his breath's withdrawal.

We put his ashes in the ground last Fall.

Doldrums

It will not do to answer *tired*
to every question you are asked:
What's up? How are you?
Is the Pope Catholic?
Would you like fries with that?

But tired is what you are
these days—sleep a siren's call
that tempts you morning, noon,
and night, though most nights
you never quite fall under
its spell, even when you spend

too many hours in bed, tempest-tossed
with ache. You even dream
of sleeping when you barely are
asleep—grateful, at least, for the support
of the pillow, the warmth of the blanket
that cocoons you in oblivion.

Outside the sky dun-gray and wind
worrying the trees, asking:
What more? What more?
And the trees answer: *The rest will come.*

Unspeakable Elegy

Brother John is gone
THE WILD MAGNOLIAS

There was the day, the world,
    then—suddenly—the news
        of you. No longer in it.

That world now one big less. One big hole
    ripped in the fabric
        of the whole of it.

There was the story of a lake, a place
    you loved, the banks of that lake, and you
        on those banks—and then you no longer.

And I cannot make myself un-imagine
    the moment of your un-being. I can't not
        ask *why?* Or *why that moment?*

Or *why not fight*—for your life, the world, the love
    of the lake, the people you loved, who love you.
        I can't make myself make that *love* past tense. I can't

not wish for you to wait, to hang on—if not forever—at least until
    that moment passes into another, so that other might pass
        into *now.* With you still being in our time being.

At least I can imagine the possibility of beauty:
    air thick with honeysuckle, the sun brilliant,
        sky azure, perhaps a few stray clouds—

all of it reflecting on the calm surface of the water,
    and birdsong and flitter—the time being late
        spring and such beauty thus common and likely—

though how *un*likely it feels that summer has arrived
    with you not here to see it. That the same sun is now
        beating down on those of us still missing

you—your laughter, your blue-green eyes as witness
    to the world I know you loved as we did you (and do)
        a world (meaning *us*, meaning *me*) that wishes

it could imagine you back into it, still and always with us.
    The hole you left forever now. Part of the whole we are.

Mother, May I

How are you? She asks every time
I call. *Are you feeling okay?*
How's the weather out there?
Reports of sunshine reassure her
all is well—or well enough.
On her end, everything is *good, good, good.*
Still kicking, not as high (both knees replaced).
On my end: *fine* and *busy* sum up life.
Minor ailments and anxieties, the death
of a friend—I keep such news to myself,
knowing she has her own quota of losses,
no need for me to add to that sad sum, even
if it's one she won't recall next time I call
to ask how things are going, what the latest
news from the doctors might be.
I do what I can; what I can't, I don't worry about—
a mantra that makes sense at any age. Like much
in life, it's easier said than done, but she repeats
the chant, and I agree that's for the best—
though worry is what prompts me, every day,
to call and ask: *How are you feeling?*
Have you eaten? Did you take your pills?
I remind her when I'll next be coming home,
so she can write the date on her calendar,
post it on the refrigerator door. *Don't work too hard,*
she says when I tell her I have work to do, have not retired
as she did after thirty years of night shifts at Bell Labs.
If she's made it to the deck or porch, she'll report
on the breeze, on the baskets of begonias she's hung,

the geraniums blooming in her window box,
perhaps the sighting of a bird or squirrel. Sometimes
she'll reminisce about long-gone neighbors, the trolley cars
that used to run when Allentown was still a place to be,
the polka bands that played the Edelweiss.
I've heard it all before, but what I do these days is listen,
answer the same question as often as it's asked, take in whatever
she still has to say. And likely say again. It's how I keep myself alive
as someone's daughter, claim my place in the diminishing space
of her memory, which holds tightly to those of us she loves
enough to know, familiar in our habits, our repetitions,
the back and forth we carry on, to keep each other carrying on.

Terminal Beauty

What is your greatest concern, the sales girl asks,
fine lines or dark circles? The once-over she gives me
makes it clear she thinks my answer should be *both*.

My layover is long, so I let her pat some goop
around my eyes and give her spiel for this miracle
product she swears she sees working
before it's even dried. *See*, she says, holding up
a magnifying mirror in which I see nothing
but my age. Magnified.

But that is not my greatest concern by a longshot.
How about the world going gleefully to hell?
Climate change? Terrorists—foreign and homegrown?
Hatred suddenly in style? She interrupts my litany
to assure me that *strong brows can make a difference*,
offers a demonstration, which I quickly decline.
Her own brows make her look perpetually surprised—
which I no longer am by much of anything,
though the eleven-lines between my eyes reveal
the worry that has weighed on me for years.

She tells me I'm in luck—there's a special offer
this week on a sampler kit that will fit in my carry-on bag.
I can begin what she calls *my new regimen*
while I'm still on the road. I say I'll think about it;
need a Starbucks before I decide, though I know
I'm going to stick with the drugstore brands
already packed in a regulation Ziploc.

I wander toward my gate—one face amidst a sea
of wandering faces, each with a destination
in mind, a history written in the hieroglyphics
of our features, our wrinkles and scars, the expressions
we have come to wear when we're too busy to care
how we appear in the eyes of others. When I catch a glimpse
of myself in a glare of glass, I decide I can live
with what I'm seeing—my late father's nose, my mother's
heavy-lidded eyes, the crooked smile I flash at my own reflection.
This is it—the best face I'll ever have to put forward.
It is no matter for great concern.

All My Dead Say Grace

They are milling about a spacious lawn,
waiting for the food I'm cooking over an open fire.
The pot is huge and black and bubbling wildly.
If I could breathe in this dream, I'm sure
whatever I'm stirring would stink.

But my dead look like they're having the time
of their lives. Some who died as strangers
are laughing together like the friends
they might have become. Couples are dancing
to music only they can hear, while a few wallflowers
who have planted themselves on the periphery
scan the sky for a distraction of birds.

The least I can do is make this meal
a good one, bring my bounty to the long table—
which appears now against a wall of arborvitae,
already laid out with bone china, fine silver,
crystal glasses ready to be raised.

My dead take their seats, join hands,
bow their heads, and whisper a word
that happens to be my name, which—
if said before eating—means *thanks*.
Which is what I am trying to say to all my dead.

Highway 2 Mirage

This is not the first time you have mistaken clouds
for hills here on the plains, where the horizon

stitches a hazy seam between sky and land
and the eye does its best to contain what appears

too vast to fathom, scouting the distance for a silo
or fence line that tells you someone claims

they own this space—though wind and weather
will often insist otherwise. There is something

to be said for persistence, the human attempt
to root as deeply as the native grass

which, in certain light, ripples like the *flat water*
they named this state after, a grand illusion—

like those clouds that, for a moment, convinced you
they were solid enough to climb.

Not Quite Nirvana

I have duct taped the Buddha's head
to his rusting body and draped him
with a string of plastic pearls pitched,
years ago, from a Mardi Gras float
into my clinging hands. The repairs
do not appear to have marred the serenity
of his repose. He continues to sit—full lotus—
between the Solomon's seal and sage.

In the neighboring bed the plastic flamingo
has weathered another winter, its pink
less gauche than when I first planted it there,
but still perched in kitschy splendor amidst a riot
of day lilies and weeds both the Buddha and I
choose to accept with equanimity—
or, perhaps in my case, sloth—

content as I feel in this moment
to do nothing but stand, statue-still,
observing the tiny agitation of a hummingbird
who flits, fleeting as a thought, into a pot of impatiens
while on the rickety fence that contains
all of us—and nothing—a jay, blue as sky,
squawks his raucous unlikely *om*.

Update on Emily

Because Death stops for everyone
and is rarely ever kind,
she writes her letters to the world—
just a piece—for the peace—of her mind.

The world—of course—rarely replies.
Not even an email or text.
When you're a fly on the wall—a Nobody—
it's a silence you learn to expect.

Yet the letters have become a way
of life—or rather—living—
as natural to her as air—and breath—
her religion—a kind of believing.

Will her words ever dazzle?
Shine—faint light—through the cracks?
Either way—in the end—
she knows we're all—called back.

The Women at the Well

Eve—*See* Genesis 2.

Noah's Wife—*See* Genesis 6–10.

Lot's Daughters—*See* Genesis 19.

Ruth—*See* The Book of Ruth.

Judith—*See* The Book of Judith.

Mary/Bethlehem—*See* Luke 1–2 and *Matthew* 1.

Anne—though not mentioned in any canonical Gospels, Saint Anne is, in Catholic tradition, the mother of Mary and thus the grandmother of Jesus.

Salome—*See* Matthew 14 and Mark 6.

The Prodigal Daughter—*See* Luke 15 for the story of the prodigal son. I imagine things might have turned out differently for a daughter. Michelle Shocked's song "Prodigal Daughter" provided some inspiration.

Pilate's Wife—*See* Matthew 27.

Martha & Mary—*See* Luke 10 and *John* 11.

Mary Magdalene—*See* Matthew 27–28, *Mark* 15–16, Luke 8 and 24, and John 19–20.

Mary/Confession & Complaint—*See* Matthew 1 and 12, Luke 1, John 2 and 19.

The Women at the Well—*See* various biblical stories, especially John 4.

Retreats & Recognitions

"Note from the Imaginary Daughter"—responds to Weldon Kees's poem "For My Daughter."

Norma Jean—a.k.a. Marilyn Monroe.

Dorothy—formerly of Kansas and Oz.

"Plot Lines"—echoes lines by Charles Dickens, Muriel Rukeyser, and Robert Browning.

"Extreme Unction"—a "final anointing" of the dying or the sick in the Catholic tradition; also known as last rites.

"Lunacy"—the poem is based on Jim Simmerman's "20 Little Poetry Projects" writing prompt.

Beholding Eye

The titles "Large Bathers," "Room in New York," and "Birthday" are also the titles of the paintings on which the poems are based. "Descending Nude" is based on Marcel Duchamp's *Nude Descending a Staircase.*

Rrose Sélavy—Marcel Duchamp signed some of his works with Rrose's name, which is a pun on *c'est la vie*—and perhaps *erros c'est la vie.*

Marcel Meets Georgia—291 was Alfred Stieglitz's Gallery in New York, and Georgia is, of course, Georgia O'Keefe.

MEAN/TIME

MEAN/TIME was also the title of an exhibition by artist Katie Merz at Fiendish Plots Gallery in Lincoln, Nebraska, in January 2016. The poem of that title, and several in the collection, served as source materials that Merz transformed into a room full of "glyphs." "A Riff on the Glyph(s)" is my response to Merz's work in progress, written specifically for the exhibit.

"Books Become Windows"—The title is from a line in the poem "Lullaby" by Valzhyna Mort.

"Still Life as Oxymoron"—Cezanne reportedly instructed his human models to "be an apple."

"Means of Transport"—echoes the line "the words are maps" from Adrienne Rich's "Diving into the Wreck."

"Dusting the Angel"—"The necessary angel" alludes to the Wallace Stevens book *The Necessary Angel: Essays on Reality and the Imagination.*

CPSIA information can be obtained
at www.ICGtesting.com
Printed in the USA
LVHW030016110821
694993LV00007B/582